Easy PC
Digital Imaging

Special thanks to Pauline; my three children, Steven, Simon and Sally; my Mum and, of course, Biffer who always lets me know when it's time to stop work and play.

Easy PC
Digital Imaging

Geoff Preston

Bernard Babani (publishing) Ltd

The Grampians

Shepherds Bush Road

London W6 7NF

www.babanibooks.com

Please note

Although every care has been taken with the production of this book to ensure that any projects, designs, modifications, and/or programs etc., contained herewith, operate in a correct and safe manner and also that the components specified are normally available in Great Britain, the Publisher and Author do not accept responsibility in any way for the failure (including fault in design) of any projects, designs, modifications, or programs to work correctly or to cause damage to any equipment that it may be connected to or used in conjunction with, or in respect of any other damage or injury that may be caused, nor do the Publishers accept responsibility in any way for the failure to obtain specified components.

Notice is also given that if any equipment that is still under warranty is modified in any way or used or connected with home-built equipment then that warranty may be void.

© BERNARD BABANI (publishing) LTD

First Published – August 2001

British Library Cataloguing in Publication Data
A catalogue record for this book is available from the British Library

ISBN 0 85934 508 4

Cover Design by Gregor Arthur
Printed and bound in Great Britain by Cox and Wyman

The Digital Revolution

Since its invention in the 19th Century, the camera's underlying technology hasn't really altered from the early wooden box constructions. Modern design and production methods, as well as the introduction of new technologies such as microelectronics, have led to cameras becoming easier to use and more reliable, and hence capable of creating much better pictures. Modern film is also better quality and more consistent, and flash technology is safer and more reliable, but the basic photographic concept remains the same: light sensitive film exposed for a fraction of a second and then developed and printed onto paper.

That was until the first major revolution in camera technology: the digital camera.

A digital camera takes a snap shot of the world through a lens in exactly the same way as a conventional camera, but the image is not stored on film, but in a solid-state device called an image sensor.

An image sensor like this VGA resolution CMOS image sensor which is produced by STMicroelectronics, lies at the heart of digital imagery.

Picture © STMicroelectronics 1999.

The image sensor is about the size of a fingernail and contains millions of tiny photosensitive diodes called photosites. Each photosite records the quality of light falling on it and stores the resulting information as a series of numbers. The numbers are then stored on either a removable disc, or an electronic memory card. The image sensor is then cleared ready for the next photograph to be taken. The images, which are stored on the camera's removable disc or memory card, can be transferred to a computer and then cleared for re-use.

A digital image is made up from millions of dots of colour called pixels which, when placed together form a recognisable image. A digital image is not dissimilar to the picture Spirit of '76 which is made from thousands of jelly beans.

© Jelly Belly Inc.

Digital camera technology has improved to the point whereby the output is almost as good as a traditional film camera. I use the term 'almost' advisedly. I personally can't see any difference, although purists will point to differences that most of us will need a magnifying glass to recognise.

The advantage of digital photography is that it's instant and free. Pictures can be viewed shortly after they've been taken, and in some cases, immediately. The longest it's likely to take to see your pictures is the time it takes you to get home or to get to a computer to transfer the pictures from camera to computer. You certainly won't need to wait several days, or even weeks to get your pictures developed. The other attractive feature is that there need be virtually no overheads. You don't have to buy film and there are no developing costs. All you need to pay for is the electricity to recharge the batteries in your camera and the cost of that is negligible. If you wish to print out any of your pictures then there is the cost of printer paper and printer ink, but these costs are far less than those involved in developing and printing films.

But you don't have to print your pictures. You can save them on your computer's hard drive or record them on a CD ROM. Again, there are small overheads, but these are insignificant when compared with the cost of film processing.

It's worth noting that high resolution digital photographs consume large quantities of disc space so if you're using your hard disc to save pictures, you'll need to be selective. But this is another strength of digital cameras over conventional film cameras. Discarding a digital image costs nothing, so you can afford to take lots of pictures of the same subject and discard all but a few of the best ones.

Access for all

Digital cameras are becoming cheaper and consequently more popular, but this book is not about taking pictures with a digital camera, or any other camera for that matter. It's about what to do with the pictures once you've shot them.

Digital Imaging

Easy PC Digital Imaging shows how to carry out basic tasks like correcting colour and light, as well as treating the dreaded red eye.

'The camera never lies.' How many times have we heard that cliché? But it's true, the camera itself doesn't lie. It can't, but if a picture is taken with a digital camera or captured from a printed page with a scanner, then there is scope to make significant alterations to it, even to the extent of combining images from two or more sources. It's then certainly possible to distort the truth and examples of this type of misrepresentation can be found throughout this book.

Working with digital pictures can be great fun and can bring a whole new dimension to your photographs. You can create some amazing effects which can look very convincing, yet paradoxically, beggar belief.

Geoff Preston

About this Book

One might be forgiven for thinking that you'll need to spend a small fortune on digital imaging software to enable you to create the stunning special effects seen on our television screens and in newspapers and magazines. Not so. All of the software referred to in this book is either free or so cheap that it can almost be regarded as free. In most cases the software is packaged with something else: if you buy a scanner, the chances are it will come with some sort of digital processing software. Even apparently unrelated programs are often supplied with software for you to use with digital images.

If you have access to the Internet, there is plenty of imaging software available as free and nearly free downloads.

Free software does not necessarily mean cheap or poor quality software. The programs featured in this book are very powerful and very capable applications, which will enable anyone to generate high quality work. It's unlikely you'll have all of the applications featured, but if you have any digital imaging software, the chances are it will be one of the applications referred to in *Easy PC Digital Imaging*. But what I've done here is, where possible, to describe processes which can be completed in most digital editing applications.

What you can do

Easy PC Digital Imaging takes the reader through the initial steps by explaining how to make corrections to common photographic defects using some of the most popular and widely available digital imaging software currently available.

It then goes on to explain how to create some amazing special effects some of which can be regularly seen in, for example, the media.

Not only does this book detail how to correct pictures and create special effects, it also shows how digital pictures can be used. Printing them on flat paper is an obvious choice, but there are other ways including greetings cards, embroidery and origami projects, all of which are described in this book. Because effects may require several techniques, the reader is referred to other sections of the book.

Please note

- Most of the software featured in this book was sourced in the United States, the largest market for computer software. Many of the menus featured in the software and reproduced in this book use US spellings. In particular, the word 'colour' is spelt without the letter 'u' but when referring to menu structures, the English spelling has been used.

- Many of the techniques described in *Easy PC Digital Imaging* can only be fully understood when another technique is mastered. Therefore, where possible, the reader is directed forward or backward in the book to a technique which needs to be understood whilst learning the technique currently being read.

  For example, to fully understand layers, you need to have a reasonable working knowledge of cutting and selecting areas, and copy and pasting principles.

- Some of the pictures printed in this book really require colour for them to be fully appreciated and for the effect being discussed to be fully understood. If you have access to the Internet you can view many of the pictures on the author's website. Full details are given on page 293.

Trademarks

Adobe, *PhotoDeluxe* and *PhotoShop* are trademarks of Adobe Systems Incorporated.

Corel, *PhotoHouse*, and *PrintHouse* are trademarks of Corel Corporation Limited.

EasyPhoto is a registered trademark of Storm Technology Inc.

GreenStreet and *GST* are trademarks of Greenstreet Technology Ltd.

Hewlett Packard and *Deskjet* are trademarks of Hewlett Packard Company

IBM and *PerfectPhoto* are trademarks of IBM Corporation.

Kodak and *Eastman* are trademarks of Eastman Software Inc.

Microsoft, *Windows*, *Windows 95*, *Windows 98* and *Windows Me* are trademarks of Microsoft Corporation.

Ulead and *PhotoImpact* are trademarks of Ulead Systems Inc.

Wacom and *Graphire* are trademarks of Wacom Co. Ltd

All other brand and product names used in this book are recognised trademarks, or registered trademarks of their respective companies. There is no intent to use any trademarks generically and readers should investigate ownership of a trademark before using it for any purpose.

Acknowledgements

Thanks to Corel Corporation, Greenstreet Technology Ltd, Kodak Ltd, Ulead Systems Inc and Wacom Co Ltd for supplying hardware and software and for providing help and support during the production of this book.

Screenshots of Corel PhotoHouse are © 2001 Corel Corporation Limited and printed with permission.

The school photographs on page 81 are © H Tempest Ltd and are used with permission.

About the Author

Geoff Preston trained as a Technology teacher in the mid 1970's, specialising in Technical Graphics, but soon became involved with computers when the Government of the day began providing them for schools.

He took up a teaching appointment as Head of Information Technology at a North London secondary school where he worked for 11 years. During this time he developed one of the first school networks covering the entire school site.

He has written about education related network issues in numerous magazines, and for 7 years was the Education Editor for a popular computer magazine.

In 1996 he was appointed Consultant Editor for InteracTive Magazine and has since been a regular contributor.

Easy PC Digital Imaging is a return to his computing roots. Much of his early work with computers was producing computer graphics to demonstrate the capability of commercial graphics applications including computer-generated animations used to explain how everyday objects work.

After 25 years in the classroom, Geoff Preston left to take up a full time career as an author.

He is an acknowledged authority on portable computers, local area networks and the Internet, and has written widely on these subjects as well as having had eight best-selling books published.

Contents

4

Printing 41

5

Brightness & Contrast 49

6

Light & Shadow 61

Hardware Choices

Computing power

Contrary to popular myth, you don't need the latest high-powered computer to be able to produce some very respectable work.

Graphic files can be very large, so you'll need space to open them so you can work on them, and space to store them when you've finished working on them. That means plenty of memory in your computer and lots of disc space.

Memory

Random Access Memory (RAM) is now very cheap and readily available. You will need at least 128Mbytes and preferably 256Mbytes. RAM can be purchased in 'slabs' as small as 32Mbytes, and you can have several slabs in your computer, space permitting. Most modern computer boards only have space for four, and sometimes only three RAM cards.

You can't have too much RAM, but it's now much cheaper than it was a few years ago. Buy large capacity slabs (64 Mbytes or larger) as you won't have space in your computer for lots of smaller cards.

Storing your pictures

The picture of the two memory slabs on the previous page is a JPEG file (see glossary of terms) which would occupy 554Kbytes of disc space. To put that into context, you would just about get three images of similar size on a floppy disc. By comparison, all the text in this book would easily fit onto the same 1.6Mbyte floppy disc.

Hard discs have got much cheaper in recent years, and their capacity has increased significantly. A second hard disc like this is now a viable option for storing pictures. There's space on this one for about 100,000 pictures of about 500Kbytes each.

Even though you may have lots of hard space, you'll need to be ruthless when it comes to storing old images which probably won't ever be used again. They can consume large amounts of space.

PCs generally have built-in control for up to four IDE devices. Your existing hard disc is one IDE device and the CD ROM drive is another which probably leaves space for two more devices. This means that if you buy a second hard disc to work alongside you existing hard disc, you probably won't need to buy anything else to make it work.

A hard disc of 20Gbytes should keep you going for a while but there are alternatives which you should consider.

Writeable CD

The problem with a hard disc is that it will eventually fill up and when it does you'll either need to erase some of the pictures or replace the whole hard disc. An alternative is to buy a CD writer. An external CD writer which connects to one of the computer's external ports (eg USB) costs a little more than a disc drive, but you can then store your pictures on writeable CD discs which are now very cheap. Using a CD writer will mean that you can build up a library of catalogued pictures with one category on each disc. A category could be a subject or a date on which the photos were taken.

Each disc can store up to about 650Mbytes. That's the equivalent of over 400 floppy discs which means you'll be able to store about 1200 pictures similar in size to the 554Kbyte picture on page 1.

Once the writable CD is full, or even at any time before it's full, you can set it so that it can be read on any PC with a standard CD ROM drive. The discs are cheap enough to post to friends so they can also view the pictures on their CD ROM drive.

The Internet

This is quite a new idea, but one which is gaining popularity. Several internet companies are offering remote disc space to save your pictures. Some companies offer a small amount of space free, but more and more companies are renting out disc space specifically to store pictures.

4 Peel Street Marsden Huddersfield HD7 6BW	**InternetCamerasDirect**™
	the sale is always on at internetcamerasdirect.co.uk
	order on line, call 01484 844 988 or fax your order to 01484 845 947

The service offered by Internet Cameras Direct at http://www.internetcamerasdirect.co.uk is typical: once you've registered you can have 50Mbytes of space to store your pictures which you can either keep private or share with others.

Pointing and Drawing

Some of the processing outlined in this book involves some close and very precise work. You'll need a pointing device with which you are comfortable and that you can control accurately. Most of the processes can be carried out with a good quality mouse.

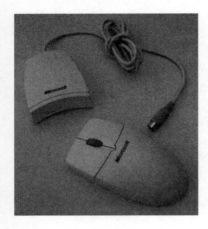

For complete freedom of movement without getting caught up, use a cordless mouse which transmits using a radio signal. There are cheaper infrared devices but these are much slower.

A cordless mouse offers much more freedom as there is no cable to get caught up. Another similar device is a rollerball (which is basically a mouse turned upside down) that sits in one place on your desk with the ball controlled with your fingers.

If you really want to do a lot of painting and retouching, there's not much to beat a graphics tablet. Of them all, the Wacom series of high resolution graphics tablets are excellent value.

The Wacom Graphire has an A6 working area (about 130mm x 95mm) and includes a cordless pen and a cordless mouse. The advantage of using the pen is that it's much more like using a real pen. You can colour and outline much more easily and more accurately than you can with a mouse because it's a much more natural way of working.

If, like me, you naturally write and draw with your left hand, but prefer to use the mouse with your right hand, the cordless pen can be placed on the left of your working area enabling you to draw and colour with your

left hand. The conventional mouse can remain on the right enabling you
to choose menu items as you always have done.

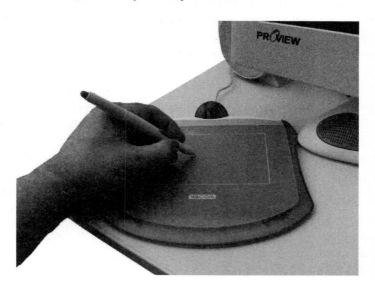

Display

Working close to a cathode ray tube monitor for long periods of time is
not to be recommended. If you do a lot of close work, one of the new
generation TFT (thin film transistor) screens are worth considering.

*TFT screens have no flicker
and are worth investing in it
you intend doing a lot of
close work.*

What else do you need?

You can begin digital imaging with surprisingly little specialised hardware, some of which is quite cheap. If you want to experiment to see if you're actually going to enjoy doing this sort of work, there are several internet sites featuring some good quality pictures which you can download. Many of the programs described in this book are supplied with a library of images for you to experiment with.

But working with other people's holiday snaps is fine up to a point, but you'll soon want work on your own photographs which will be more personal to you and feature scenes and people you know. There are basically two ways of getting your own images into a computer.

Scanner

When digital imaging is mentioned, a scanner is not usually the first thing that comes to mind, but if you're setting up on a budget, this is probably your best choice. The price of scanners has been in free-fall for several years and where they were once hundreds of pounds, you can now get a very good quality scanner for less than £100. Most models are A4 size so can be used to scan a very large picture. Try to get one with the highest resolution possible. The higher the resolution, the better quality your pictures will be.

If you already have a good film camera, a scanner makes sense because you'll be able to scan old pictures from the family album as well as new photographs taken with a traditional camera.

A scanner may well be more versatile for your particular needs. Apart from scanning pictures, it can also scan written (typed) documents and with the right software (which again is often supplied with the scanner) the text on the page can be converted into editable text which you can drop into your word processor.

If you want to work with old photographs or slides, it may be worth considering a picture scanner which is specifically designed to scan printed photos.

Digital Camera

If you're really serious about digital picture processing, then you're going need a digital camera. The cost of digital cameras has also fallen considerably, but a good quality model is still quite expensive: compared to traditional film cameras, they are about 2 to 4 times the price when comparing like with like.

A good quality digital camera featuring through the lens viewing (the digital equivalent of a single lens reflex camera) will cost several hundred pounds, but there are cheaper alternatives.

As with most consumer electronics, you get what you pay for. Digital cameras are now available for less than £50. Clearly these are not going to be as good as a camera cost 10 times as much, but you can nevertheless get some very acceptable pictures from them.

More expensive cameras have a small LCD panel which enables you to view the picture you have just taken, or in some cases, view the picture you're just about to take. This is a feature worth having as you can immediately see how good the picture is and whether to keep it or discard it. This is something that can't be done with a conventional film camera.

Most digital cameras now use removable memory cards to save the pictures, although some use floppy discs. These are either 3½" floppies which can be taken out of the camera and inserted into the computer's floppy disc drive, or purpose designed discs which are much smaller.

Disc based cameras are a popular alternative to cameras which store their images on memory cards. These discs can store up to 50 pictures depending on size and resolution.

Webcam

You can get some quite good pictures from so-called webcams. These small cameras are now very cheap, but are permanently tethered to the computer making them non-portable.

The pictures produced by webcams tend to be smaller and lower resolution than other digital cameras. This is because their main purpose is to create pictures to upload to the Internet.

If you have a laptop computer you can buy a small camera which is designed to be connected to the computer's PCMCIA socket. These produce similar quality pictures to webcams, but because they're portable by virtue of the fact they're connected to a portable computer, you're not restricted to taking pictures in one place.

Memory cards

If you have a film camera and you go on holiday or on a photographing expedition with it, the one thing you need to take is an adequate supply of rolls of film. If you have a digital camera you won't be taking film, but you will need a sufficient supply of appropriate media to store your pictures.

The two most popular media are Compact Flash and Smart Media.

Compact Flash and Smart Media are common storage media used in cameras to store digital pictures. Both are available in a variety of sizes and, as is often the case, the larger the size the cheaper it is per Mbyte.

Compact Flash is slightly more expensive but because it is enclosed in a case, it is more robust. Even so, care should be taken not to drop memory cards or handle them roughly. Sony's Memory Stick has similar properties but is used only with Sony products.

The number of pictures which can be stored on a memory card will depend on the size of the card, the size of the pictures and their resolution. As a guide, the number of 1712x1368 pixel, with 16 million colour pictures that can be stored on a 32Mbyte card is about 55. (If such a picture was printed full size at 72 dots per inch, you would need paper 604mm x 482mm which is larger than A2 size paper.)

If 55 is not enough you have two choices. The first is to buy more memory cards. They are supplied in a neat protective case and can be easily changed when full. In fact, it's a great deal easier to change a memory card than it is to change film rolls in many conventional cameras.

The second alternative is to use a portable computer to store your pictures. You won't need lots of cables, just one piece of very cheap hardware which is shown on page 12.

Copying to your computer

One reason for using a digital camera is so that you can transfer your pictures to a computer for long term storage or for editing. All digital cameras are supplied with a means of transferring pictures from your camera to your computer, but some systems work better than others.

Most digital cameras are supplied with a lead to connect it to the computer so that images from the camera can be 'downloaded' into the computer. In many cases these cables use the computer's serial port which, whilst being cheap, simple to set up and reliable in operation, is very slow. Anyone with such a system may care to consider some alternatives.

Card readers are available for both Compact Flash and Smart Media memory cards. When installed (usually through the computer's high speed USB port) they appear on the computer as an additional removable disc drive with similar drive properties to a floppy disc or CD ROM drive. The memory card in inserted into the card reader and files can be moved to the computer's hard disc just as you would if it were a floppy disc.

This card reader accepts both Compact Flash and Smart Media. Transferring files from the camera to the computer is much faster than using the serial lead supplied with many cameras.

This solution also requires no special software to download the images. Simply insert the memory card in the reader and read them on your computer. You can load them directly into a photo editing application or copy onto the computer's hard disc.

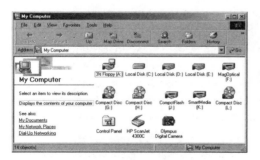

The card reader appears as another disc drive. Because this particular reader accepts two types of memory card, it appears as two disc drives.

The SmartMedia or CompactFlash folder containing the pictures can be opened just as any other folder, and files can be dragged from this folder to another like My Pictures, or if required, pictures can be copied from the computer to the memory card.

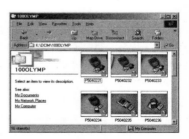

To enable you to see thumbnails of the pictures rather than icons representing picture files, go to **View** on the menubar at the top of the filer window (the window which opened when you clicked on the card reader's icon) and choose **Thumbnail**. Note that if you choose this option the window with take slightly longer to open.

If you have a laptop computer it will probably be fitted with a PCMCIA slot (sometimes referred to as a credit card slot). If you have such a port then you can buy a PCMCIA card reader that accepts either Compact Flash or Smart Media, but not both.

These readers are quite cheap, particularly the one for Compact Flash which can frequently be found for less that £10. They work in exactly the same way as the USB reader, appearing on the computer as an extra disc drive. Opening the drive reveals a window containing the files which can be dragged into another window.

This solution means that even when you're away from home you can take just one or two memory cards with you and transfer pictures from your digital camera onto the hard disc of your laptop computer.

Printers

It's debatable whether the improvement in digital cameras has led to better printers or the other way round. Only a few years ago you would have to pay several hundred pounds for a printer that is good enough to output photographs. Now you can get a good photo-quality printer for about £100.

What to look for

Ideally, you need a printer that carries a label saying that it is photo-quality. In addition, it should be able to print on a variety of papers, (including plain paper) and it uses at least two ink cartridges, one for black the other for colours. (Printers that mix black from all the other colours are expensive to run and they tend to output muddy green rather than black.)

As home colour printers go, they don't get much better than this Hewlett Packard DeskJet model which, with the correct ink cartridges, can also print on transparent acetate film for use on overhead projectors.

The latest development in inkjet printers are those which have memory card readers built in so that the memory card can be taken from a digital camera and plugged directly into the printer so that the pictures can be printed without going through a computer. The advantage with this type of printer is that you can print any or all pictures on a memory card immediately, but it does bypass the possibility on any form of picture editing – clearly the printer will only print the photograph that it's given on the memory card. You can, of course, transfer an edited image from the computer back onto the memory card but if the picture is already in the computer you might as well print it from there.

Running a colour inkjet printer can be quite expensive, but it's still nowhere near the cost of developing and printing photographic film. Some printer cartridges can be refilled but care should be taken if you intend doing this. Don't attempt to do it yourself but go instead to a reputable company that specialise in re-manufacturing laser toner and inkjet cartridges. Any foreign particles in the ink could irreparably damage the print head rendering the printer useless.

A better solution might be to buy a slightly more expensive printer which can be fitted with larger ink cartridges which can produce more printouts.

Paper

A good inkjet printer should be able to print on a variety of media, including plain paper. However, even the best printers will produce much better copies if printed on treated paper.

Several printer manufacturers produce treated inkjet paper in a variety of thicknesses or weights. The standard print paper is $80g/m^2$ and for most purposes this will be perfectly adequate. Inkjet paper is available with either a matt or glossy finish and both will give excellent results.

For better quality work you might consider thicker such as $140g/m^2$ or even $170g/m^2$. These papers are significantly more expensive than the thinner papers but they are sold in smaller quantities so you don't need to spend a lot in one go. Typically, $80g/m^2$ paper is sold by the ream (500 sheets) whereas the thicker grades can be bought in packs of 50 or 25 sheets, or sometimes even less.

If you want something really special, Ryman produce a range of good high quality A4 papers including $190g/m^2$ paper which is textured to look like canvas.

Photo size paper

If you don't want to print on A4 sheets, you can now buy postcard sized sheets ready cut which will fit most printers and even folded card for greetings cards.

There are several sizes available and are very good quality but quite expensive.

If you intend using any of these papers you need to ensure everything is set up exactly as you want it as mistakes are expensive. If you're not sure, it might be worth printing out in draft quality on ordinary paper first.

You will, no doubt, build up a small stock of paper. But be aware that some treated papers degrade in light and so the papers should always be kept in their packs and preferably stored in a drawer or cupboard so they are kept flat and away from bright light.

Software Choices

Digital editing

Where digital images really score over conventional film images is that you can perform some sophisticated editing on them. Once the domain of specialists who could charge whatever they liked, editing digital images is now within everyone's scope. Individuals working from home can now correct basic photographic errors and produce professional looking special effects on their pictures and use them in a variety of ways.

Some of the software for editing digital images is very expensive, but there are several which are free. I've always believed that something that's free is usually worth what you've paid for it. But, in this case at least, it's not so. Some of these programs can produce some superb work which is at least as good, if not better than expensive 'professional' digital imaging applications

At the last count, I had over a dozen photo editing programs, all of which were given free when purchasing something else. In many cases, these are 'cut-down' versions of larger programs and have been supplied to 'whet the appetite' and encourage you to buy the full version. But even after being 'cut-down' they are still very powerful and you can do a great deal of very fancy work with them.

Cut-down versions of applications usually carry the term SE (special edition) or Lite. In some cases the 'free' version has noticeably fewer features than the full size version: some of effects or functions may be missing, or there might not be as many example images as the full size version. But this is not always the case. I have one 'cut-down' application that was free but appears to be identical in every respect to the 'full' version costing over £100.

Free software

All of the photo editing applications have strengths and weaknesses. This applies to the full, paid-for versions as well as the free, cut-down ones. I use most of the applications, but I use five more than any other and frequently find that some projects require more than one of the applications to complete. If a particular project has three stages, I often find that I complete the first stage with one application, save the work, open it and do the second stage in another application before transferring the work into yet another one for completion. The trick is to find the elements of each program that you are most comfortable with and use those to complete your work.

The applications mainly (but not exclusively) referred to in this book are...

PhotoImpact SE by **Ulead**. I had this photo editing application for several months before I realised just how good it is. I needed an HTML editor to create web pages and so bought *HoTMetaL* by ULead. On the same disc were several utilities including *PhotoImpact SE*.

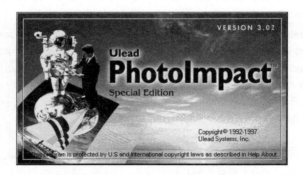

The latest version of *PhotoImpact* is available as a limited-life free download from http://www.ulead.com/pi/trial.htm. Once downloaded, you can use it for 30 days free of charge but if you wish to keep it, you will have to pay for it. Even if you do decide to keep it, the cost is quite small. *PhotoImpact* has a huge range of features which can be fine tuned to create just the effect you're looking for. All effects are categorised so selection is easy, but if you prefer you can choose to pick from a single menu listing all of them.

PhotoEditor by **Microsoft**. This is part of Microsoft's *Office* suite and has the same 'feel' as other *Office* applications. Like many photo editing applications, you can scan directly into *PhotoEditor*.

The application is not overloaded with features, but the effects that it offers, it does very well.

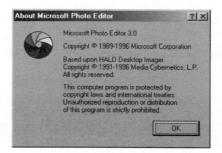

This application is particularly useful for preparing an image for inclusion in other *Office* documents.

PhotoDeluxe Home Edition by **Adobe**. Adobe is well known for its photo editing applications and *PhotoDeluxe* has many of the features of its more expensive stable-mate, *PhotoShop*. *PhotoDeluxe* was a surprise addition to the software supplied with a scanner.

The features can be accessed via the conventional menu system, but *PhotoDeluxe* also has its own menu system which is more graphic in appearance and provides a degree of help as you work through a particular effect.

PhotoHouse by **Corel**. When I needed a second scanner I chose a Hewlett Packard model and on the installation disc were three extra programs including Corel's brilliant *PhotoHouse*. *PhotoHouse* is actually part of *PrintHouse* (also included on the HP Scanning software disc) which offers enhanced image printing.

Like *PhotoDeluxe*, *PhotoHouse* has an alternative to the conventional Windows menu system. **Guided Activities** is a panel which resides on the side on the main *PhotoHouse* window and provides guidance for the various functions and effects available in the application. If Guided Activities is not active, a floating window called the **Notebook** is available which does a similar job. Each function or effect has its own 'page' of the notebook which replaces the conventional dialogs as well as offering guidance.

PerfectPhoto by **IBM**. I recently bought a new computer which came with several programs, most of which were discarded very quickly. I almost did the same with this program but I thought I would have a look to see what it does. It was just as well I did because this image editing application from IBM has some excellent features, especially the text facility which includes several clever effects.

The message is simple: look carefully at all software you acquire and make sure there's nothing hiding away. It might be a piece of rubbish, but it could easily be a gold nugget.

When installed, *PerfectPhoto* places a hidden toolbar at the top left of the screen enabling you to easily recall the picture editor as well as the Gallery and Album, which are part of the application.

PerfectPhoto's features can be accessed via the usual menu system but it also has its own menu system which can be used to access the various effects and functions.

Each of the eight buttons, when clicked, opens a collection of icons below the buttons which provide access to the various features of the software.

Other useful programs

Other free programs which may be of use are...

Picture It! by **Microsoft**. If you use (or used) Windows 98, you may have bought the optional extension, *98Plus!* On the 98 Plus! CD are several programs including *Picture It!*. If you just want to do some simple cropping and basic error correction, this application works well.

Paint by **Microsoft**. Although not really designed for photo imaging, *Paint*, which is one of the programs that can be installed *with Microsoft Windows*, can be used because it can load many of the bit-mapped image formats. For photo editing it's very limited, but for some tasks like adding speech bubbles and individual pixel editing, it can be quite effective.

Imaging for Windows by **Kodak**. This program is supplied with Windows and is excellent for use with a scanner and for re-sizing pictures. It also has one of the easiest annotation tools allowing the user to add captions quickly and easily, but most importantly, consistently.

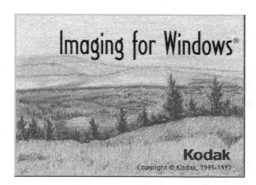

If you want to produce fancy special effects this is not the choice but for basic image transformation, this is a very easy application to use.

PhotoShop LE by **Adobe**. This program was bundled with a digital camera. The full version is regarded by many as the ultimate professional digital imaging tool and although the LE version doesn't have all the features, it is still a very capable application.

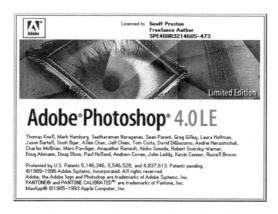

If you're considering buying the full version of *PhotoShop*, try using the LE version first.

Going cheap

Whilst most of the programs described in this book are bundled with other products, there are some which must be paid for, but the price is so small they can almost be regarded as free and are a valuable addition to your armoury of digital photo editing tools.

PhotoFX and **PhotoFX2** by **Greenstreet Technology**. These applications are brilliantly simple and really cheap, but can produce some really good effects very easily. *PhotoFX* costs less than £5 and is a good basic photo-editor, whilst the slightly more expensive *PhotoFX2* includes all the features of *PhotoFX* with a few extra special effects.

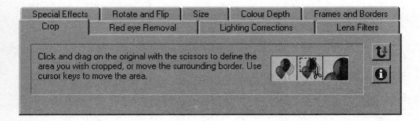

All the effects are accessed via the tabs at the top of the window. At the bottom of the window are two panels containing the original picture and the results of any modifications.

The use of free software

Although the software described in this book is effectively a free gift, it doesn't mean you can do what you like with it. All software has a copyright, including that which is given for no charge. You may not make copies of the software, nor may you lend or give it to anyone else. The manufacturers have granted you permission to use their software, but they still own it, even if they have elected not to make a charge for its use.

Please respect the owner's copyright.

Loading & Saving

Loading pictures

Modern PC applications offer three distinct ways of loading or opening a document. (A document is any file, be it a picture, drawing, text file, etc.) The usual way is to locate the document from within the application by selecting it from a menu, but it is also possible to locate a document from the filer window and force the document to launch the application or drag the document into the application.

Open a document

A document can be loaded into an application which is running by clicking the left mouse button over the 🖻 icon or by moving the mouse pointer to **File** at the top left of the menubar and clicking the left mouse button which will open a drop down menu.

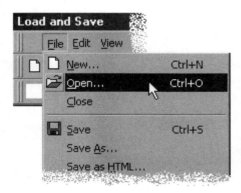

The second entry at the top of the menu is **Open...** and clicking the left mouse button on this entry will open a dialog from which you may choose the document you wish to work on.

You can locate the document you wish to work on by opening the folders. If you want to back-track, click on the 🗁 icon which will take you up a level in the directory. When you've located the document you wish to work with, click on it once and then click on the **Open** button.

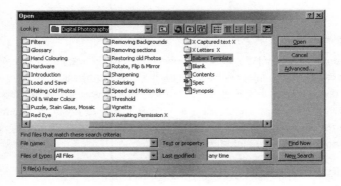

Drag and drop

A second way of opening a document is to locate the document you wish to use and then drag it from the filer window and drop it into the application's window.

The proviso is that the application you are attempting to load with a document is actually capable of working with the document in its current format. For example, if you attempt to drag a MS *Word* document into

Imaging, you'll get an error message telling you that you can't load the document because its format is either invalid or not supported.

Run the document

The third method of opening a document into a application is to run it as if it were an application. If you move the mouse pointer onto a file icon in a filer window and run the document in the same way as you would normally run an application (by either double or single clicking (depending how your computer is set up) with the left mouse button), the document will launch the application that was used to create it. For example, if you move the mouse pointer onto a 🖼 icon, running it will launch the *Paint* application *and* open the document you clicked on.

This feature is made even more useful because you can declare which application you want to be opened when a particular icon is clicked.

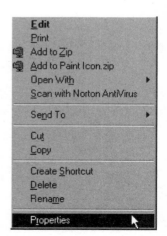

To change the application which is launched when a file is loaded, move to the file icon in a filer window and with the mouse pointer over the file, click the right hand mouse button once to open a menu.

Move down to the bottom entry, **Properties**, and click the left mouse button to select it.

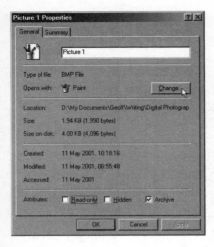

A dialog will open headed *filename* **Properties**.

This dialog gives a range of information about the selected file including size and date it was accessed.

On the right is a button labelled **Change**. Clicking on this will open another dialog...

... headed **Open with**.

It may take a while to open because it will list all the currently installed applications.

Move to the one you now want the chosen filetype to open and click **OK**.

Beware, this window will display all installed applications including those which will not work with the chosen filetype.

Once you have chosen the application you want to open with the icon you chose, all documents carrying that icon will also launch that application until you go through the same procedure to choose another application to be launched with the filetype.

Variations

All applications support this method of loading documents, but some applications also have their own system which the software developers feel have advantages over the 'standard' method.

PerfectPhoto uses different icons but is similar to the conventional method. Click on **Start** and choose the **Open** icon which is on the extreme left, next to the camera.

PhotoDeluxe uses bold icons which is entirely in keeping with the type of program it is. Go to **Get & Fix Photo** and a range of icons appears just below the menubar. Click on **Get Photo** and a drop down menu opens. Click on **Open file...** and the standard dialog is displayed, from where the file is chosen.

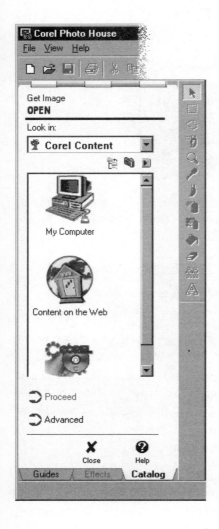

As with many features of Corel's *PhotoHouse*, opening a file begins with a click on the standard **Open file** icon on the menubar. The **Guided Activities** panel on the left part of the main window opens and the file can be chosen by clicking on the arrow alongside the panel containing the legend **Corel Content**. This lists a variety of locations which are also duplicated below (**My Computer, Content on the Web**, etc.) and can also be clicked on. This opens all the locations on your computer where suitable files could reside. From there you can navigate through the various folders until you arrive at the location where the file you wish to work on is stored.

Clicking on the file icon will open it.

If you wish to go back, the icons above the main panel will take you either back to the beginning or back one level.

Clicking **Advanced** opens a filer window from where files can also be chosen.

Saving a document

At the top of many applications is a 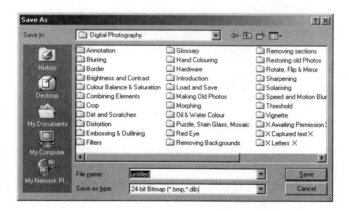 icon and clicking on this will save the document (with the current filename) into the location from whence it came. Alternatively, clicking on **File** on the menubar and choosing **Save** from the drop down menu will have exactly the same effect. This, of course, assumes that the document has a name and its location is known. If not, clicking on the disc icon or choosing **Save** from the menu will open the **Save as** dialog.

You'll need to enter a suitable name and decide on a location before clicking on the **Save** button to save it.

You may also have a choice of the format of the document. If you wish to save it in a different format than the default, click the arrow to the right of the **Save as type** panel. Choose the filetype you wish to use from the list and then click **Save**.

Filenames

When a picture has been taken with a digital camera it is usually given a default filename (100021.jpg is typical of the sort of name that many cameras generate). The trouble with this name is that it tells you nothing at all about what the subject of the picture is, nor when it was taken. Clearly you can open the document to find out what it's about and you can look at the **Properties** to find out when it was created, but it is better to have the information in front of you rather than having to hunt for it. You can display thumbnails (see page 11) but this option will make the filer window take longer to open.

There are several ways to overcome this problem, my preferred method is to create a folder whose name is the date and the documents inside can be renamed in a more appropriate way.

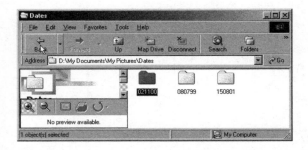

When creating folders you must be aware of the restrictions regarding the characters that can be used for naming documents and folders. Because of these restrictions, using the date as a folder name will have to be in the format similar to 020301 without **\ / : * ? " < > |** between the groups of digits as these characters are not allowed.

If you adopt the American format for the date (*month/day/year* rather than our system *day/month/year*) and you use four digits for the year, they'll be arranged in chronological order when you sort the folders by name.

Changing names

It may be that you want to keep original photos (ie the ones taken with your camera or scanner) and modified ones. If this is the case, instead of clicking the **Save** icon, choose **File** from the menubar and choose **Save as...** from the drop down menu. You can then change the name and/or location and/or filetype. Changing any one of these will preserve the original document whilst generating a new document. In future, choosing **Save** will save the new filename and location.

General tips

Some of the processing outlined in this book requires several steps. You are strongly advised to save each step as a different file. Save the original photograph with a name in the normal way, but after each step has been completed, save it with a variation of that name. Eg if your original picture was called *Parliament*, save the edited versions as *Parliament (1)*, *Parliament (2)*, etc.

If something goes wrong, you can refer to an earlier version although it's also worth remembering that in most cases, pressing **CTRL Z** will undo your last action.

New files

Most applications have a 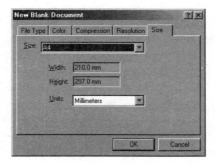 icon on the toolbar which, when clicked on, will create a new document. Those that don't feature this icon have the menu equivalent: click on **File** on the menubar and choose **New** from the drop down menu. Before the new document can be displayed, you'll need to declare some of the parameters for it. Each program handles this in a slightly different way, but in general you'll need to enter the size of the blank document and the filetype and possibly other information like the resolution.

Kodak's *Imaging* opens a dialog with 5 tabs. All the options have been completed with default values, some of which may need to be changed. You can determine the size of the new document in either inches, millimetres or pixels.

You also choose the number of colours (or the number of grey shades used) and determine the resolution including a custom resolution when the document is created. Remember, the more colours you choose to have, the more memory the resulting file will consume, both in the computer whilst you're working on it and when it's stored on a disc. Physical size and filetype also have a bearing on the amount of memory a file will consume. It may not be an issue, but you can easily create a file which is too large to fit on a 1.6 Mbyte floppy disc.

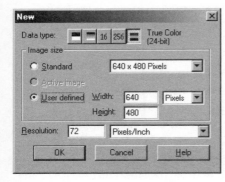

PhotoImpact has a similar number of options, but they're all contained within one dialog without using tabs to divide up the information.

The default size for the new document is one of the standard digital camera sizes. Most of the default settings are likely to be what most people will need most frequently.

PerfectPhoto offers a similar dialog, again with fairly useful default settings which are likely to be adequate for most uses.

An additional feature is the opportunity to define a background colour.

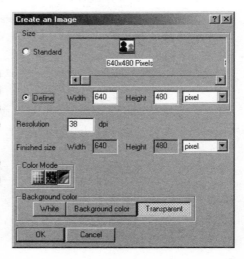

PhotoDeluxe has a very useful feature in that it tells you what size the image will be based on the current settings. You also have to specify a name at this stage.

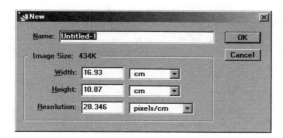

Microsoft's *PhotoEditor* also shows what the size of the file will be based on its current settings. Both the *PhotoDeluxe* and the *PhotoEditor* dialogs are among the easiest dialogs to use for creating a new file as they both include all the information that is vital at this stage, and little else.

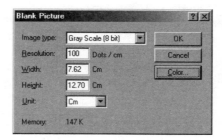

You can choose the size of the picture in any of the three standard units (inches, centimetres and pixels), the resolution and the number of colours or grey shades required.

You can also define the background colour. Click the **Colour** button and a palette will open. Click on the colour you want to use and click the **OK** button.

Clicking on the **New** icon in Corel's *PhotoHouse* opens the **Guided Activities** panel on the left of the main window. There you can use the default settings or alter some or all of them.

Apart from entering dimensions to determine the size of your new blank document, you can choose from a range of standard sizes. This feature means you don't need to remember the size of postcards, folded cards or standard photograph sizes.

PhotoHouse also shows you the filesize based on the current settings.

When you've got the parameters for the new file as you want them, click on **Apply** to create the blank document. With all other applications, click on the **OK** button on the **New** dialog to create the file.

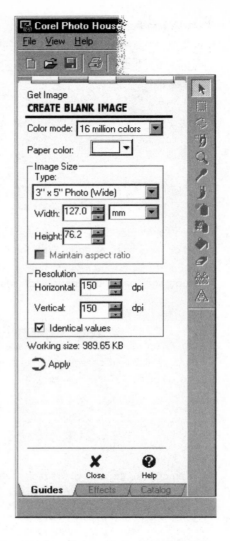

Once a new document has been created, save it before attempting to work on it. It's better to find out at this stage (when you've got a blank document) that you haven't got enough disc space or the place where you wanted to save it is full.

Filetypes

The most common file format for digital photographs is JPEG (.jpg), although Windows Bitmap format (.bmp) is frequently used. What both of these filetypes cannot support are transparent areas and information about layers and selections.

If your work contains selected areas and you save in a format which does not support selected areas, all the selections will be merged into the main picture, as this message from *PhotoImpact* confirms...

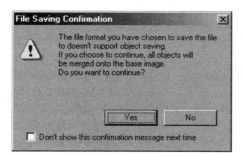

A file saved as a UFO file will have its own icon which, when double-clicked, will launch PhotoImpact.

PhotoImpact supports its own filetype called UFO (Ulead File for Objects) which will preserve all selections. (Refer to the Glossary of Terms of page 277 for a description of Objects.) You can test this for

yourself. Open a file into *PhotoImpact*, select a small area, copy it (**CTRL C**) and paste it (**CTRL V**) somewhere else on the picture. If you then save the picture as a UFO file, close it down and then re-open it, you should still be able to move the selection around. If you try this with a Windows Bitmap or JPEG file you'll find that the selected area will become part of the main picture, and more important, the piece of the picture that was underneath it will be lost.

Other file formats can be tested in the same way to check they will save all the information. In general, if the file format you are attempting to use doesn't support features you've built into the file, then you'll be told.

PhotoHouse uses Corel's CPS format which supports selections and layers.

 Adobe's *PhotoDeluxe* uses a file format called PDD which saves information about the layers of a picture edited in *PhotoDeluxe*.

Adobe's PhotoShop also uses PDD files but also supports a variation of this filetype called PSD.

 PerfectPhoto's file format includes the data about layers used in *PerfectPhoto* files.

Final version

Using these file formats is recommended when editing your work and even when you've finished editing, you should still keep your files in these versions in case you do want to do some adjustment later. But if you intend sending your picture to someone else, or embedding it in a text document, then you should also save it in a more common format. Indeed, the text editor you're using may not support one of the special file formats which have been developed by the software companies who produce digital imaging software.

It's also worth noting that these special file formats create files which are much larger than some of the more widely used formats. This is obviously going to be the case as the files include not only the main picture, but possibly several sections of the picture.

For final work use JPEG or Windows Bitmap (or possibly TIFF) which are compact and can be read by many applications.

Importing

Some applications can import pictures in a variety of file formats which will be added to the existing document. *PhotoHouse* is typical. Click on **File** on the menubar and choose **Import...** from the drop down menu. This opens the Import dialog which looks similar to *PhotoHouse*'s Save dialog.

Navigate through the files until you find the file you want to import. If the file is not present in the list, then it is not in a compatible format and so cannot be imported.

When you have found the file you want to add to your existing picture, click on it and then click **Proceed**.

When the file is imported it will be to the same scale as the current picture is displayed in. It can be positioned anywhere in the picture and provided you save it in a suitable format (ie one that supports selections) you will still be able to reposition it in the picture when you reload it.

Gradually you will build up a library of images which you can use over and over again.

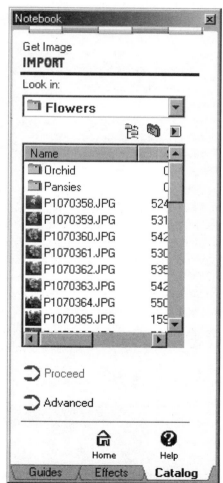

Exporting

Sometimes referred to as **Save as...**, this option enables you to save your picture in a different format to that normally used by the application. This option can be found by clicking **File** on the menubar and choosing either **Export** or **Save as...** from the drop down menu.

Some applications then display a dialog similar to the save dialog in which you can choose the name and the filetype you wish to save the file as.

Choosing **Export** in *PhotoImpact* opens a sub menu from which you can choose to save the file in either GIF or JPEG format. These so-called SmartSavers allow you to perform numerous operations on the file as it is saved. These include compressing it and reducing the number of colours: both designed to reduce the size of the resulting file.

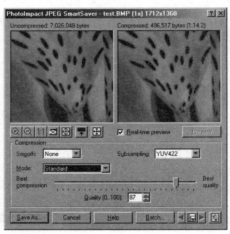

In *PerfectPhoto*, **Export** sends the picture to its own gallery which is a sort of reference area for picture information enabling them to be easily located. *PhotoDeluxe* is similar in that it can send its picture information to a gallery called **My Photos**. This feature is covered in detail in the section Galleries and Albums on page 257.

4

Printing

A hard copy

At some point you will want to print your pictures. You probably won't be printing all of them, but you'll certainly want some of them printed.

Basic setup

The basic printer setup determines which printer you intend using (if you have more than one), the quality of the printout and the size (and sometimes type) or paper you're using. The settings are entered in a dialog which will vary in content depending on which printer you have installed on your computer system. The diagrams here refer to a Hewlett Packard 970Cxi.

The Print Setup dialog can usually be found by clicking on **File** on the menubar and choosing **Print** from the drop down menu.

This feature is one of the most inconsistent features of Windows software. In some software, choosing **Print** from the file menu opens a totally different dialog. In *PhotoImpact*, for example, a dialog opens which has a button labelled **Printer...** .

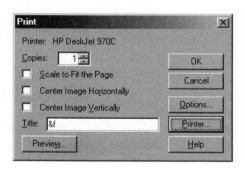

Clicking this button will then open the Print Setup dialog shown on the next page.

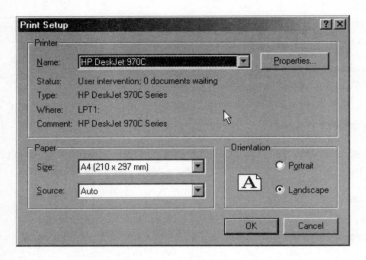

The first step when you've found the Print Setup dialog is to choose the printer from the drop down list in the **Name:** panel. Then choose the paper orientation: Landscape or Portrait. Landscape has the longest edge horizontal and is the format you will need if your picture was taken with a camera held normally. You should then choose the paper size. A4 is the most common size, but most printers can accept a range of smaller sizes, typically as small as 127mm x 77mm.

Print quality

Clicking on the **Properties...** button gives the user the opportunity to select the quality of print which will often be determined by the paper you're using.

Most printer set-ups default to plain, untreated A4 paper. For the best images you should use coated paper of which there are several types, frequently only distinguished by price. If you are using plain paper, it's usually best to keep to an average print quality as the higher qualities will tend to flood the paper with ink. High quality papers are designed to cope with this, but cheap photocopy quality paper will become sodden and will buckle and smudge making a mess of the printout, and in extreme cases, the printer too.

If you want a high quality image, choose high quality paper and select the paper type from the drop down list.

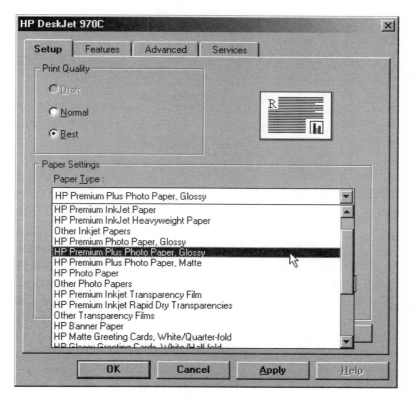

Choose the best print quality and if the dialog features an Economy mode, switch it off.

Custom paper size

Although you can choose the paper size from the Print Setup dialog, if you choose a custom size (ie a size not listed) then you can specify the exact size in the Properties dialog.

When you choose **User Defined Paper Size** from the drop down list, a small dialog opens into which you can enter the size of the paper. Always enter the smallest dimension in the panel labelled **Width**.

Failure to observe this will mean the Landscape / Portrait choice will work the wrong way round. (ie choosing Landscape will print portrait and vice versa.)

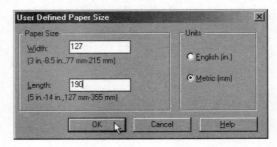

Other options

The dialogs associated with printer setup will have other settings depending on the exact printer being used. Most can be left as they are, although you should ensure that if there is a Photo Quality mode, it's switched on.

Getting it to fit

Some programs are notoriously difficult to get the picture to fit to the size of paper you're trying to print to. One of the easiest is *PhotoImpact*.

Clicking on the **Print Preview** 🔲 icon on the toolbar opens a new window with a white rectangle representing the paper size you have chosen in its selected orientation. Just inside the representation of the paper is a red rectangle denoting the printer's limits.

Note that most printers can't print to the very edge of the page and the margin is often larger on one end – the end that is pulled into the printer first.

The easiest way to ensure the picture fits onto the paper is to click **Options** on the toolbar and select **Fit to Page**. If you want to centre the picture on the page, choose **Centre Horizontally** and **Centre Vertically**.

Note that these options centre the picture on the paper, not to the printing limits on the paper.

These options should, however, be used with a degree of care. If the picture is larger than the page you're trying to print on, **Fit to Page** is an easy way to ensure all of the picture gets onto the paper. If, on the other hand, the picture is much smaller than the page, using the **Fit to Page** option is not recommended as in can lead to pixelation. (See the Glossary on page 277 for an explanation of pixelation.)

Free resize

If the printer preview has a free resize, like *PhotoImpact*, it should be used with extreme caution as the picture's aspect ratio could be lost resulting in proportions changing. (eg, people looking too short and fat, or too tall and thin.)

Clicking the **Resize** icon on the Print Preview window will place eight nodes around the picture. Dragging one of the nodes will alter the size of the printout, although not the picture in the editor which will remain unchanged.

To preserve the aspect ratio, most software will allow you to hold down the **Shift** key whilst dragging. The picture can also be positioned on the page by hand, usually by placing the mouse pointer near the centre of the picture and dragging.

If the picture is only slightly larger than the paper, you can drag the picture around the page and position it so that the subject will be on the page and the only edges of the picture fall outside the printer's printing limits.

This picture is about 20% too large for A4 paper but it has been positioned by hand to get the best composition without resizing. The picture will be printed to the limits that the printer will allow, which in many cases will mean that there will be a larger margin on one side due to the fact that the printer needs a good 10mm to pull the paper into position.

Paper setup

Many inkjet printers print on the side of the paper that is face down. Ensure you put the paper in the correct way round as most treated inkjet paper is designed to be printed on one side only. When all the settings have been set, you can click the print icon on the toolbar, or from the Print button in any of the dialogs. Of them all, **CTRL P** followed by **Return** seems to be the quickest.

Brightness & Contrast

Why adjustment may be necessary

Sometimes, a photograph paints a gloomy picture. It's not necessarily because the subject is gloomy but may be because the wrong settings were uses when the photograph was taken, or more likely in this country, it was a gloomy day.

One of the principal functions of digital photo editing programs is to adjust the brightness and contrast of the picture. All but one of the programs featured in this book offer this function, but with different degrees of effectiveness.

Controls

In most cases you have two controls: one for brightness and one for contrast. The trick is to get the best combination or balance of the two to give the best possible results.

PhotoDeluxe offers the simplest solution having just those two controls (brightness and contrast) which can be dragged back and forth to alter the photo to get the desired effect.

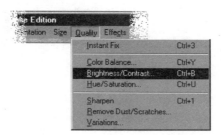

The controls are accessed by clicking on **Quality** on the menubar and choosing **Brightness/Contrast...** from the drop down menu.

*The dialog begins with both controls set to zero. Ensure the **Preview** box is ticked if you want to see the alterations on the photograph as the controls are moved.*

Whenever one of the controls is moved, the effect can be seen on the photograph. If you prefer, you may enter values into the panel on the right instead of dragging the sliders.

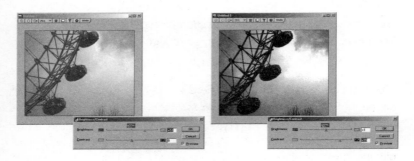

Increasing the brightness only results in a washed out picture whilst increasing only the contrast makes it difficult to see much of the detail. On this particular picture, neither results are satisfactory, but for some pictures this could produce an interesting effect.

To get a better balance, a combination of brightness and contrast is required. How much of each will to some extent be dependent on what you're trying to achieve.

The picture of the London Eye was taken late afternoon on a fairly grey day. The original picture is shown on the previous page and captures the greyness of the day with some dark clouds moving in on what turned out to be a rather wet evening.

This picture has had some brightness and a small amount of contrast added and has warmed the picture making it look as though it was a much brighter day than it actually was. Too much brightness will make the picture look washed out but if you want to try to make a brighter picture, more brightness can be added as long as the contrast is increased by a similar amount.

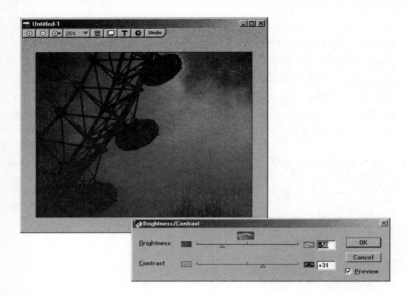

A similar amount of contrast, but with a negative amount of brightness will make the picture look as though it was taken much later in the evening.

Microsoft's *PhotoEditor* has similar controls but also features Gamma control as well as providing the option of working the colours individually.

This option is accessed in *PhotoEditor* by clicking on **Image** on the menubar and choosing **Balance...** from the drop down menu.

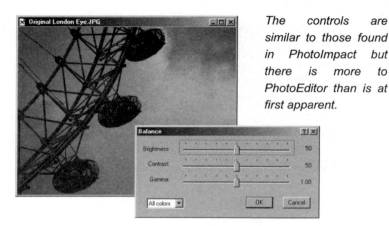

The controls are similar to those found in PhotoImpact but there is more to PhotoEditor than is at first apparent.

The controls are set to centre regardless of what image is being edited and brightness and contrast are then altered by dragging the slider. The current values are shown on the right of the dialog.

Gamma

The Gamma control changes the contrast in the dark areas of the image. Just a small increase in **Gamma** has transformed this picture.

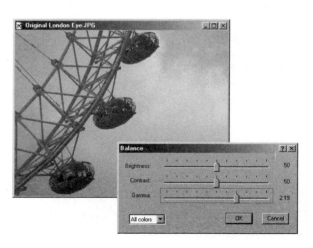

Intensity

A similar effect to *PhotoEditor*'s Gamma is Intensity found in Corel's *PhotoHouse*.

Intensity alters the brightness of the light pixels more than the darker pixels. Increasing the intensity will make the lighter tones more vivid but will maintain the darkness of the darker tones.

As with all *PhotoHouse* effects, you can access brightness and contrast adjustment by going through the Guided Activities or by clicking on **Effects** on the menubar, going to **Color Effects** on the drop down menu and choosing **Brightness/Contrast...** from the sub menu.

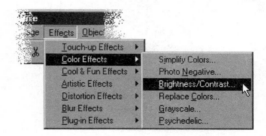

The controls for Brightness, Contrast and Intensity appear on the left hand panel. You can either drag the sliders, enter a number in the panels on the right or increment the numbers by clicking on the up/down arrows above and below the numbers.

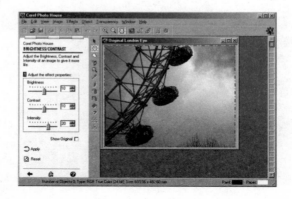

By increasing the intensity, the white cloud has become brighter, but the darker areas have hardly changed.

RGB control

As well as working on the whole image, *PhotoEditor* can be set to adjust the values for each of the primary colours: Red, Green and Blue.

The same picture of the London Eye has been made to look as though it had been taken against a red sky. Whilst this picture still looks 'correct' (in the sense that it looks as though it could have been taken without any after-editing), individual RGB control can be used to get some very strange-looking effects.

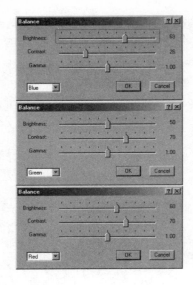

It's not possible to fully appreciate the picture on the previous page unless it's viewed in colour. For those wishing to duplicate the effect used on the picture on the previous page, the settings are …

Simple control

PhotoPerfect offers a more visual method of adjusting the brightness and contrast. To locate the Brightness and Contrast dialog, click on **Image** on the menubar and then choose **Brightness/contrast…** from the drop down menu.

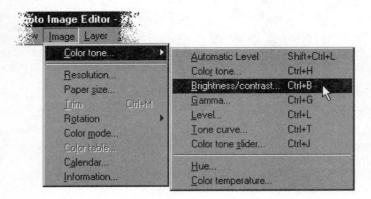

The dialog shows nine variations of the image you're currently working on, which the current setting being the one in the middle.

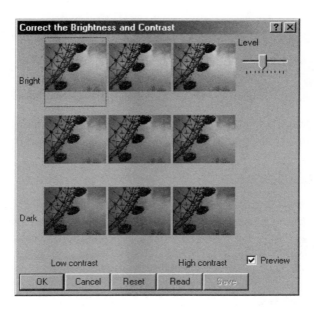

The top left is bright with low contrast, the top right is bright with high contrast, the bottom left is dark with low contrast and the bottom right is dark with high contrast. The overall brightness and contrast can be adjusted with the single slider at the top of the dialog. Clearly this offers less control than some of the other programs, but you have a better chance of getting the overall balance correct.

When you have the setting you want, click on the image in the dialog that you like to apply those settings to the picture.

Automatic adjustment

If you prefer to do even less work yourself, some programs offer fully automatic adjustment of brightness and contrast, and occasionally, some other elements like colour intensity.

PhotoEditor features **Autobalance** whilst *PhotoDeluxe* has **Instant Fix**. There's not a great deal to choose between them.

In the centre is the original picture of the London Eye flanked by the image adjusted using Autobalance (left) and Instant Fix (right).

Selected area

So far, all the brightness and contrast adjustment has been to the whole picture, but most applications will allow you to choose an area of the picture and apply the alterations to the selected area whilst leaving the unselected area untouched. There is more information about selecting areas in the section on page 131.

Rectangular area

Selecting a rectangular area will enable you to highlight the area to draw attention to it. In *PhotoHouse*, simply drag from top left to bottom right to choose the area you wish to adjust. From there on, adjusting the brightness and contrast is exactly the same as if it were the whole image being worked on.

Irregular area

Corel's *PhotoHouse* allows you to select irregular areas in two ways: a freehand selection tool which you can draw around an area to select it and a brush to allow you to 'colour in' an area.

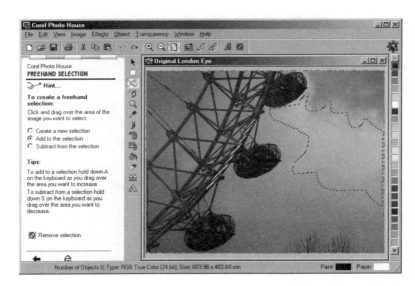

Both tools can be found in centre toolbar between the Guided Activities panel and the main drawing area.

Which one you choose will be largely dependent on precisely what you want to do. As a guide, small or thin areas like the framework of the London Eye are usually best brushed in, whilst larger areas are best outlined with the freehand selection tool.

Once the area has been selected, brightness and contrast can be applied to that area without any other part of the picture being affected.

When using this tool, it is often best to enlarge the picture so that you can better see the exact edges of the area you're trying to select.

The magic wand featured in *PhotoImpact* and *PerfectPhoto* enable irregular areas to be selected automatically. This is a particularly useful feature which will enable you to select complicated areas very quickly and very accurately.

In the example of the picture of the London Eye, the magic wand tool is chosen from the toolbox (in the case of *PerfectPicture*) or from the left hand toolbar (in the case of *PhotoImpact*). Move the mouse pointer to the area you wish to select and click the left mouse button. The area will be selected and as can be clearly seen from the picture, hard edges like the framework of the London Eye are followed, but also areas where colour fades and merges into another colour are outlined. If brightness and contrast are to be applied to this area, the values used should be noted so that other selected areas can be adjusted by the same or similar amount.

Light & Shadow

Highlights

Not all of us have sophisticated lighting for our pictures, but many digital imaging applications make a good attempt at reproducing clever lighting tricks or emphasising the highlights already present.

The square bottle was photographed in poor light but even so you can detect highlights at the bottom of the neck and the top of the flat sides. Emphasising these and adding some extra highlight to the nearest corner gives the impression of much stronger light reflecting off the surface.

This effect was carried out using the highlight facility in *PerfectPhoto*, although it could have been done in *PhotoImpact*.

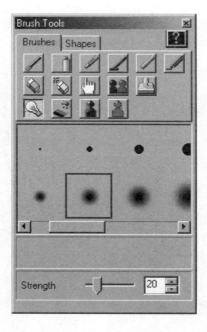

The dialog in *PerfectPhoto* which contains this effect is found by clicking on **View** on the menubar and choosing **Brush Tools...** from the drop down menu. Choose the light bulb button to add highlights and the shadow button to apply shadows to a picture.

Always begin with the strength setting quite low and use a small pattern with faded edges. Adjustments to the settings can be made as you begin working.

Shadows

Shadows can be added in several ways but one of the simplest methods can be found in *PhotoImpact*. You'll need to select the object first and then click the right hand mouse button to open a menu and choose **Convert to Object**. Having made the selection into an object, right click again and this time choose **Add Shadow...** to open the dialog.

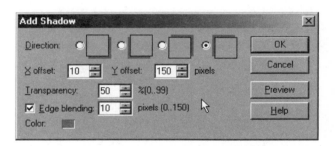

You can choose the direction you want the shadow to go in and the amount, which is determined by the X and Y offsets. Choose the shadow colour (dark grey is usually the safest) and the degree of transparency. The more transparent the shadow is, the more detail you will be able to see through the shadow.

PerfectPhoto has an almost identical method of adding shadows. The main difference is that with *PhotoImpact* you have to enter the offset values as numbers whereas *PerfectPhoto* has a graphic which you can drag to get the position correct.

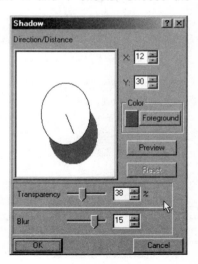

Although this is quite a simple and effective method of applying shadows, it has some limitations; the main one being that the shadow can only appear to fall on a vertical surface.

Both *PerfectPhoto* and *PhotoImpact* create the shadow as a new object on a new layer. (For a full description of layers, read the section on page 177.) The important feature of a layer is that it can be worked on independently of the rest of the picture. If the shadow is selected it can be processed in several ways, including shearing: sliding one side of a rectangle whilst keeping the opposite side in the same position.

This is exactly the same picture as shown on the opposite page except that the shadow has been sheared. The shadow is now falling on the floor, rather than the wall.

Lighting effects

If you have *PhotoDeluxe* you can light an object after you've taken the picture. This clever effect can be found by clicking on **Effects** on the menubar, going to **Render** on the drop down menu and choosing **Lighting Effects...** from the sub menu.

When the dialog is displayed you first need to choose the type of light or lights that are to illuminate the subject of your photograph. There are nine options including a torch (which is described by its American term: a flashlight), two intersecting lights and multiple lights with different coloured filters.

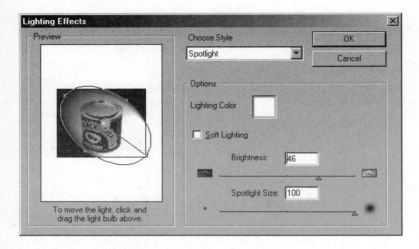

You can choose the lighting colour, brightness and size of the light(s). The bulb in the centre of the left hand panel can be dragged to the position that best suits the picture and the spread of the beam can be altered by dragging the nodes on the four edges of the ellipse. If you choose multiple lights, you get multiple bulbs and multiple ellipses to adjust.

Colour

What is colour?

Lighting is all-important when taking photographs and a good photographer will consider the amount of light and the quality of light when taking a photograph. When light hits a surface, some is absorbed and some is reflected. It is the reflected light that forms colours.

There are an infinite number of colours but humans can only detect colours with a wavelength which falls between about 380 nanometres (red) and about 750 nanometres (violet). Theoretically we can see any and every colour in this range but age, health and lighting conditions means that at best, we can only distinguish between 10 and 16 million colours.

When working with digital colour you should remember that there are limits on the number of colours that can be displayed. This will depend on the quality of the monitor you are using, the amount of memory your computer has and the format the photograph is in.

For home use, 24 bit True colour (see the Glossary on page 277) is more than adequate. In this mode, your computer can handle 16.7 million colours. By comparison, some professional imaging equipment can handle as much as 70 billion colours.

The difficulty we have when describing the effects of subtle colour change is that pictures displayed in a book which is printed in black and white don't often adequately illustrate the particular effect being discussed.

Colour balance

Adjusting the balance of a picture or part of a picture can have a dramatic effect on a picture. It can give a dull, dreary picture a brightness which can disguise poor lighting.

PhotoImpact has two devices for adjusting the balance of colour – one requires the user to make decisions, but the other is a smart adjustment which the software works out for itself.

Both are available from the same dialog which is opened by clicking on **Format** on the menubar and choosing **Colour Balance...** from the drop down menu. The manual system is the one displayed first and takes the form of nine thumbnail pictures, each with a varying degree of colour balance.

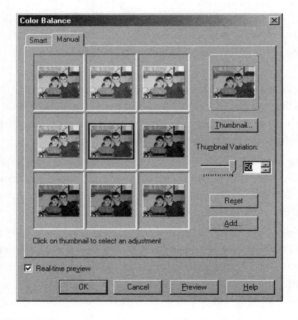

The overall value can be set by the slider on the right. The value entered here is its maximum to enable as much change as possible to

be shown on a black and white illustration. A value of half that is usually more appropriate.

You can select the thumbnail that most suits your needs by simply clicking on it and then clicking the **OK** button.

The Smart alternative takes a different approach. Here you are asked to pick a colour from anywhere on the picture that should be grey. The mouse pointer changes to an eye-dropper and the current value of the pixel underneath the eye-dropper is displayed under the main picture on the right.

A shade of grey (whatever shade it may be) should have the same values for Red, Green and Blue (RGB). Click the left mouse button when the eye-dropper is over what should be a grey pixel and click the **OK** button. The picture should then be automatically adjusted for balance.

PerfectPhoto and *PhotoDeluxe* have a similar dialog where the overall colours can be balanced by choosing the best effect from a series of variations.

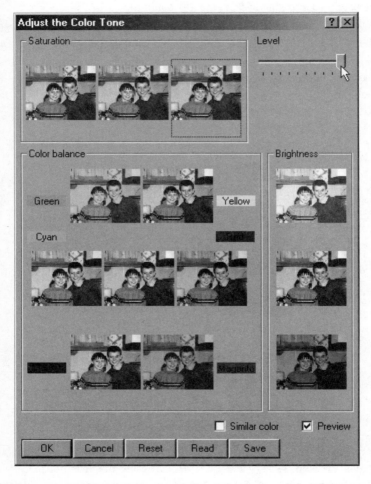

This dialog (from *PerfectPhoto*) can be found by clicking on **Image** on the menubar, going to **Colour Tone...** on the drop down menu and choosing **Colour Tone** from the sub menu.

Colour components

Some software refers to Hue, Saturation and Lightness. Hue is the colour, Saturation is the strength of colour and Lightness is the amount of black or white in the picture. *PhotoDeluxe* provides a dialog with sliders so that either the whole picture or a selected area can be adjusted.

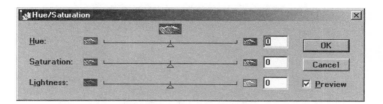

Dragging the Hue slider to the left or right passes the picture through the available spectrum. For example, the pine cupboard door in the background is a straw-yellow colour.

Dragging the slider to the left changes the colour of the door to blue going through red and purple. Moving the slider to the right changes the colour to blue but this time the change is via yellow and then green.

Saturation changes the amount of colour or tint in a picture. Moving the pointer to the left reduces the amount of colour. As you move the pointer further to the left, the tint becomes duller. When the pointer reaches the extreme left, you'll have a greyscale picture. Moving the slider to the right adds more and more colour until you're left with a picture which is completely flooded with colour.

Even when viewed in black and white, it can be clearly seen how the picture has taken on a mottled appearance when compared with the identical picture on the previous page.

The Lightness slider controls the amount of black and white in a picture. If the pointer is moved to the extreme left, you'll get nothing but a white rectangle. Move the pointer to the other extreme and the picture will become totally black. Places in between will give a lighter or darker picture.

You can use all of these effects to change the overall colour of a picture, or selected area(s) within a picture.

Light temperature

Many digital imaging applications provide filters which will attempt to change the light that the picture was originally shot in.

PerfectPhoto has a series of options which attempts to automatically compensate for poorly lit pictures.

You can choose these by clicking **Effects** on the menubar...

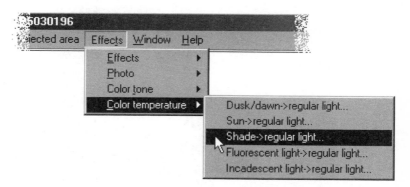

... or by clicking **Image** on the menubar, going to **Colour Tone...** on the drop down menu and selecting **Colour Temperature...** from the sub menu.

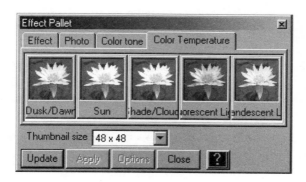

Each effect attempts to correct poor light by changing the colour balance.

Tone curve

For total control over the colour, including the ability to alter the colours within a given range, some applications provide a tone curve or tone map like this from *PerfectPhoto*.

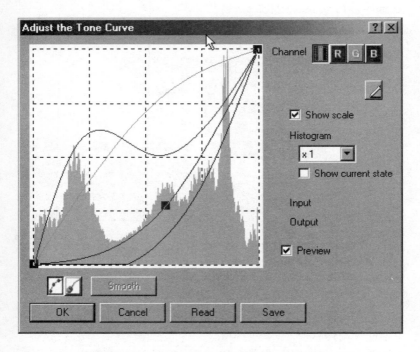

With a tone curve, not only can you adjust, say the reds, but you can determine which reds to adjust. The advantage of this option is that you can make radical alterations to one range of colours with a minimum effect on others.

Clicking the **Channel** button on the top right adjusts all colours, but choosing the individual colours (**R**, **G** and **B**) allows you to adjust that colour only.

Changing colour

Some photo editing applications offer colour changers which will allow you to replace all pixels of one colour with another colour. Some of these work quite well, but a better way of changing colours within a picture is to select the item you wish to change and then apply one of the effects previously described in this section.

To fully understand this effect, you'll need to read the section on selecting areas on page 131. Simon's pullover is green, although when the photograph was taken it was grey. Changing its colour is not simply a case of painting it with another colour. If you do that the shadows and highlights that make it

look three-dimensional, together with the other features that make it look knitted, will be lost.

If you want to change the colour of a section of a picture, begin by marking around the pullover with a freehand selection tool. Next, open a colour tone dialog. This one used here is from *PerfectPhoto*.

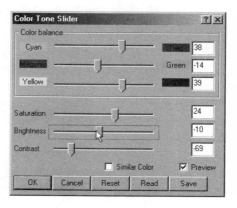

The sliders can be adjusted so that the pullover can be given any colour, but the shadows and highlights present in the original will still be seen.

No colour

Most digital imaging applications offer a range of colour change effects which involve removing colour from the picture. Two of the most useful are Sepia and Half Tone.

Sepia

This effect attempts to reproduce old pictures by converting them into a wash known as Sepia. A Sepia picture is much the same as a greyscale picture except that instead of shades of grey, it has shades of red/brown. If your software doesn't offer this effect, you can reproduce it by converting the picture to greyscale (Saturation 0) and then adding a red/brown tint to it.

Half Tone

PerfectPhoto features this effect which is similar to the technique black and white newspapers use to print photographs. If you look carefully, the picture is made up of black dots – the spacing of which provides the detail.

Posterising

What is posterising?

This is an interesting feature not found in all programs. The idea is simply to reduce the number of colours in the photograph.

PhotoDeluxe offers this feature and it may be found by clicking on **Effects** on the menubar, going to **Artistic...** on the drop down menu and choosing **Posterize** (or Posterise) from the sub menu. A dialog opens into which you must enter a value between 2 and 255.

If you prefer *PhotoEditor*, choose **Effects** from the menubar and then **Posterize** from the drop down menu. This will open a dialog into which you can enter the number of bits per pixel, and which colour or colours to work on.

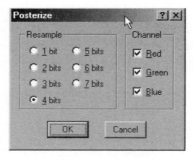

You can get some interesting effects with this feature in *PhotoEditor*. You'll see these effects used a great deal in advertising.

On the left is 1 bit, with red and blue selected and green removed, whilst on the right, both blue and green have been removed. Some of the combinations are barely different from the original. These pictures are featured on the website. See page 293.

Threshold

If the idea of this effect is to reduce the colours, the ultimate conclusion must be just two colours. There are variations of this feature in other programs, but without doubt the most straightforward versions can be found in Adobe's *PhotoShop LE* and IBM's *PerfectPhoto*. Placing a threshold on a picture simply turns it black and white only, without any grey shades. All shades above a given level become white, whilst all those below become black.

In *Photoshop LE* click on **Image** on the menubar, go to **Adjust...** on the drop down menu and choose **Threshold** from the sub menu to open a dialog.

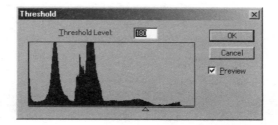

Either enter a value between 1 and 255 in the panel, or drag the arrow at the bottom of the graph to adjust the threshold level. When a picture is subjected to this treatment you need to carefully locate the exact threshold point. Too high and the picture will be too black, too low and it will be too white.

With care, a picture can be converted so that the subject is still recognisable. Portraits generally work best. It's amazing how much detail can be removed, and yet the subject can still be recognised.

The threshold feature in Adobe *PhotoShop LE* doesn't actually produce a true Black and White only picture. This is because the program anti-aliases the image which produces a much smoother appearance. (See Anti-Aliasing in the Glossary on page 277).

Output

If you're going to print a picture like this, you really need to spend some time tidying it up first. The effect is very well implemented in *PhotoShop LE*, but there will almost certainly be odd black pixels in the areas that should be white and white pixels where there should be black. Magnify the image by at least 4, and work through the picture with the pencil tool to correct stray pixels.

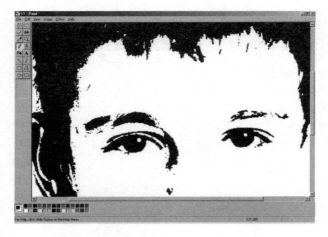

Of all the programs which can do this, *Paint* (which is part of the Windows 95/98/ME suite) is as good as any. Open the picture in *Paint*, select the pencil from the toolbar on the left and work through the picture clicking the left hand button (black) to cover up any white pixels and the right button (white) to cover any unwanted black pixels.

Sewing

An interesting way of outputting this type of picture is to an embroidery machine. The Aisin POEM is an embroidery machine specifically designed for connection to a PC. In simple terms, you provide a

picture and POEM will embroider it. The restriction is that the picture needs to be simple.

If you're going to try this, you'll need to carefully prepare your picture. You'll also need to carefully choose your picture as some work better than others.

The original scanned photographs look similar in composition, but Simon is looking directly at the camera whilst you can see more of the side of Sally's face. This will have an effect on the final output.

After scanning the photograph, load it into *PhotoShop LE* and select a suitable threshold to produce a black and white image.

Remember, there will be some grey pixels in the picture (from the anti-aliasing) and these will need to be removed. There are several ways to remove the grey pixels on the edges of the image, but probably the easiest way is to save the picture from *PhotoShop* as a .bmp file, load it into *Paint* and save it from there as a monochrome bitmap.

Whilst in *Paint*, it will be worth going round the image removing some of the odd pixels that may have occurred because of fuzzy areas from the original image, like hair.

If you don't have a program which outputs a two colour picture, you can try saving a coloured picture from *Paint* as a monochrome bitmap. You won't have the control that *PhotoShop LE* offers, but you can get some good results.

After outputting from *Paint* as a monochrome bitmap, you should be left with just two colours – black and white. You can embroider the picture in this format, but you will get better results if you 'tell' the embroidery machine the order in which to embroider the various elements of the picture. The way this is done is to add colour to each of the various shapes which make up the picture. The colours have no significance other than as a means of controlling the process and are not reflected in the final output.

If you don't do this, you find the POEM will embroider part of the mouth, then a bit of the ear and then part of the eye, before going back to the mouth. Adding colours to the pattern provides some control over the way the embroidery is done.

When you're reducing the amount of information in a picture to this level, you need a really good picture to begin with. Because Sally's head is turned slightly there was a shadow under her chin which showed the shape of her face. The shadow was removed in the threshold process and consequently the shape of her face has changed.

Simon's full face picture is much more suitable for this type of treatment. Interestingly, I could recognise Simon just by the two black shapes that were his eyes and eyebrows. With the correct photo it's amazing how much information can be removed without the subject becoming unrecognisable.

If you can borrow a computer controlled embroidery machine this is an effective and unusual treatment of a picture.

The school photographs of Simon and Sally are © H Tempest Ltd and are used with permission.

Hand Colouring

Improving features

Time gets the better of all of us. Wrinkles, lines and other defects begin to take hold as age takes its toll. But with a little time and some careful selection of tools and colours it is possible to put the clock back. Or push it forward. (It is with deep regret, however, that I have to announce that this process only works on photographs.)

I have to be careful what I write, because this is my wife. Apart from blurring the background, the top picture is untouched. The bottom picture has been air-brushed to remove some of the lines around the corner of the mouth and above the upper lip. The lower cheek has been slightly reshaped just in front of the earring and the heavy shadow which runs from the corner of the nose towards to corner of the mouth has been lightened slightly. The crows feet around the eyes have been removed and some of the neck lines have been removed.

This was all done using the colour picker and airbrush in *PhotoImpact*, but could just as easily be done in almost any of the featured image editing applications. The trick is to be patient, make slight alterations and remember that if the work is heading in the wrong direction, **CTRL Z** undoes the last action.

A graphics tablet is by far the best tool to use for this task as you can work in much the same way as you would if you were using a real airbrush. Begin with the largest alteration first. This is the line that runs

from the corner of the mouth towards the bottom left of the picture. Use the eye-dropper to sample the colour alongside the shadow. There will be a colour chart just below the menubar which tells you which colour you've picked. Click around the area you're working on to find the lightest colour. Now, select

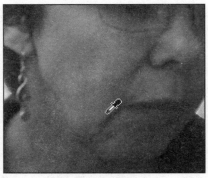

the airbrush by clicking on the icon. When the airbrush has been selected a panel of options will be displayed under the menubar.

For most purposes, a round spray pattern should be chosen and a radius of 30 pixels will be about right. Set the transparency quite high so that the spray will alter the colour gradually. The rest of the options can remain as they are.

When you begin, set the picture to full size, not larger, and work in long(ish) strokes, releasing the button at the end of each stroke just as you would with a real airbrush to avoid build-ups of colour at the ends of each stroke.

After finishing one piece, move to another area but choose the colour from near to the area you're working in.

The same technique can be used to experiment in other ways. I'm not a fan of young girls wearing makeup, but when performing on stage it is necessary. You can use this technique to experiment with makeup combinations.

Once again, I have to be careful what I write as this time it's my daughter. This transformation was carried out using PerfectPhoto. The photograph at the top is untouched: the bottom photograph has had the works. The purple eye shadow was applied first with a small airbrush and then smudged with the finger tool. The lipstick was applied with the pencil, as was the eye-liner. The blusher doesn't show up in black and white, but it was applied using the airbrush with near maximum transparency.

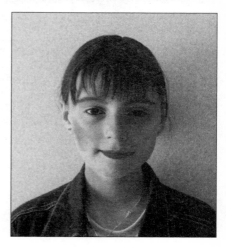

Again, it's best to work with the picture no larger than full size and if possible, use a graphics tablet which works especially well for work such as this as, like a real pencil, it's pressure sensitive so the harder you press the darker the colour.

The brush tools in *PerfectPhoto* can be found by clicking on **View** on the menubar and choosing **Brush Tools...** from the drop down menu. Like *PhotoImpact*, you can set the transparency value and for this project it should be set quite high to ensure the underlying detail, such as the lines on the lips, is not lost.

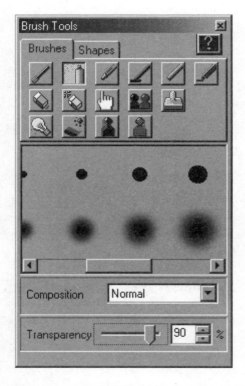

Each tool has its own selection of 'brush' patterns which are basically different shapes, sometimes with the option of a hard or soft edge. Which you will use will depend on what you are doing. In most cases, circular is more useful than other shapes. When choosing a tool, think about the tool that is used in the real world and choose something similar.

Removing areas

This sounds like a simple process, and it can be. But it can also be so difficult as to be virtually impossible. Removing an object from a picture is fine so long as you know what is behind it.

This picture of part of the London skyline was taken from the South Bank. At the time the photo was taken, this was the clearest section of skyline with just one crane towering above. Removing the crane is a relatively easy task because it's obvious what's behind it. Sky.

This task was completed using *PhotoHouse*, but it could have been completed in virtually any imaging application, including *Paint*. The technique is simple. Choose the colour of the sky near to the crane and use a small airbrush to spray out the offending image.

For this task, it's worthwhile enlarging the picture slightly before commencing and a mask may be useful. Read the section on masks on page 99.

Having selected the colour and then the airbrush, use short strokes to remove the offending item, releasing the spray button at the end of each stroke. When you get close to the building, enlarge the photograph so you can get close to the building without removing any of it. This is one of the relatively few occasions when a square spray is better

Smudging

A smudger is a now little used slang word for a photographer. In particular, seaside photographers who would take an unsolicited picture and provide you with a ticket which you used to claim your photograph later on in the day, were known as smudgers. It is therefore entirely appropriate that the word should feature in the vocabulary of digital image processing.

Most good image editing software includes a smudge tool which is used to blend one colour into another. It is analogous to blending pencil with your finger to produce a graduated (dark to light) shading.

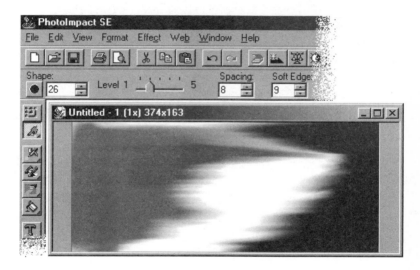

PhotoImpact's smudging tool is one of the best with several adjustments available including the shape of the smudging tool, the size and the degree to which it works. Once the tool has been selected, move the mouse pointer into an area of colour and drag the mouse (press and hold left mouse button) to blend one colour into another. Different shape tools, hard or soft edge tools and the degree of softness all have an effect on the way the tool works and the effect you get.

Although you can use this process to produce some interesting effects, its main purpose is for retouching photos.

Cleaning up a mess

You get called upon to do all sorts of odd jobs. This sundial has clearly been visited by birds who have left a mark on one of the corners. The picture cannot be re-taken and so the only thing to do is to clean up the mess.

This task was completed in *PhotoImpact* using two tools: Smudge and airbrush. The smudge tool is used to cover up the blemish by 'pushing' surrounding colour into it. Working from each side towards the centre, the mark can gradually be replaced with the correct colour, or to be more precise, something that approximates the correct colour.

Some of the detail around the blemish is going to be lost. This is unavoidable.

It doesn't look very promising at this stage, but now the area is approximately the same colour, it can be blended with an airbrush which should be set with a medium transparency value.

Although it doesn't look very good when shown at four times its normal size, when shown at normal size it will look fine.

The detail cannot be completely restored without an enormous amount of time but it can be approximated sufficiently well so that when shown full size it will be passable.

The detail is simply a curved line drawn with the thinnest crayon possible. Use the eyedropper tool to capture the correct shade from the circle near to where the gap is and very carefully freehand draw the line. If you miss slightly, you can touch it up by selecting a crayon with colour to match the background.

If you feel in need of adding additional detail, you could try adding a few other lines, but by the time you get the picture to the correct size, you're unlikely to see them.

Filling white space

Another use for the smudge tool is to correct errors or inaccuracies in your work or, in some cases, in the software.

If you cut out a piece of a picture and try to replace it, you may find that it doesn't fit exactly.

This picture of Simon standing in a rather unlikely position needs to be removed but later returned to the same position. It's almost the same as if it were cut from a piece of wood: the shape will be too small for the hole because the saw has actually removed some of the wood.

Having cut out a shape and separated them so you're left with…

… putting them back together might not give the desired effect.

Note the white area around Simon which looks like an aura. Sometimes enlarging the shape slightly will successfully cover the white area but with a complicated shape like this, any alteration in size could make it worse.

The way to correct the error is to replace the white area with colour which is the same as the surrounding area.

When using a smudge tool, try the take into account the background shapes and try to work with them. Immediately behind where Simon is standing is a wooden fence made up from vertical slats. When using the smudge tool in this area, drag down from the fence into the white space and although only the colour will be blended into the white space previously occupied by Simon, you'll get the effect of the vertical lines of the fence moving into the area. The dark lines between the panels, for example, will also be blended in the white space.

Similarly, the kerb which is behind where his knees will be, is roughly horizontal and it is in that direction that you should work. Remember, you're moving colour into the white space so always drag into the space but don't go too far into the coloured area. You'll only need to blend a few pixels.

Simon has now been replaced in the same position as he was, but this time he has the car between himself and the fence. The background immediately around him has been blended into the space behind ensuring there is no white glow around him.

Masking

Protection

It's common practice to protect areas which are close to the areas on which you are working. This applies in the real world as well as when working with digital photographs. Spraying paint is a prime example. If you're using a spray gun, aerosol can or airbrush, you need to protect the bits you don't want sprayed using some form of mask. Even painting window frames with a brush requires a good deal of care, or copious quantities of masking to avoid getting paint on the glass.

Of the featured applications in this book, only *PhotoImpact* has a tool which is actually called Mask, but all of the applications will allow you to protect areas using one of the selection tools.

Selection

Most effects which are discussed in this book operate on either the whole picture or, if a selection has been made, on the selected area or areas only. This is effectively a mask and will allow you to work on one area (the selected area) without affecting anything close by.

This is part of a picture of Biffer sitting on a beige carpet. To change the colour of the carpet to, say, green, could be done by swapping colours. The only problem is that the shade of carpet is too similar to Biffer's fur colour, meaning that he too could end up green. The way to do it is to select the carpet and give it a green filter.

Having selected the carpet, a green filter was placed over the picture but it only worked on the selected area. The result was a beige dog on a green carpet. In fact the chair in the top left and the table leg in the bottom right also got a green tint. Had they been selected out they too would have remained their original colour.

PhotoImpact's Mask Brush enables you to paint a mask. Click on the Mask Brush icon 🖉 on the toolbar and a coloured transparent mask will cover the whole picture which isn't already selected.

The toolbar will inherit some new icons which will allow the user to choose the shape and size of the mask brush, whether to add to the existing selection or subtract from it, the colour of the mask and whether it has a soft edge like a spray or a hard edge like a brush.

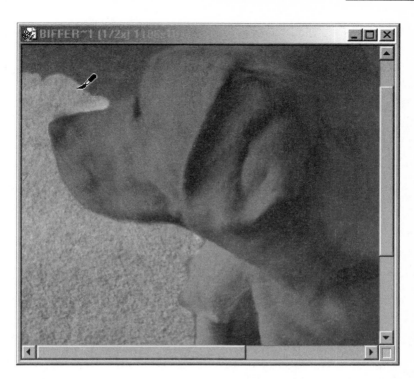

The mask has covered the whole picture and the brush is now being used to remove the mask from the carpet. If you run into the area you want the mask to cover (in this case, Biffer), either choose **Subtract** from the Mask toolbar on press the right hand mouse button as you paint. This will replace the area of the mask that was accidentally removed. (If you're using a graphics tablet, pressing the button whilst shaping the mask will have the same effect as **Subtract**.)

When the area you want has been marked on the mask, click the **Select** button on the toolbar to turn the mask into a selection. If you want to put the mask back, click on the Mask icon again and the mask will be replaced on all the areas not selected.

Just to prove that it works, I chose a dark colour spray with no transparency and a very large spray area and sprayed across the whole picture. Only the area outside the mask was affected.

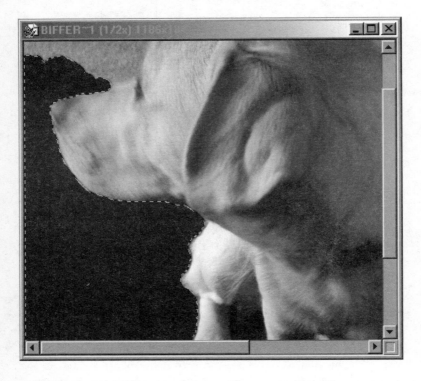

A more detailed description of selecting can be found on page 131.

Sharpening

Re-focus

If your picture taking ability is as good as mine, this is a technique with which you will soon become familiar. With modern cameras with automatic focus and exposure, it's quite difficult to get pictures which are out of focus, but occasionally it can happen and sharpening may be able to correct it.

As with all effects, the computer cannot add information that is not already there so a sharpened picture is never going to be as good as a picture that was taken correctly in the first place.

Most imaging applications have some form of sharpening facility, but they do vary in the way they are operated and the results they give. It's impossible to determine which is better as some work better on some pictures, whilst other applications work better for other pictures.

PhotoImpact's sharpen dialog can be found by clicking **Effect** on the menubar, going to **Blur & Sharpen** on the drop down menu and choosing **Sharpen...** from the sub menu.

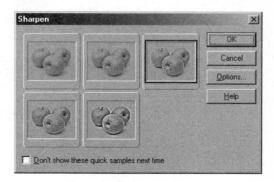

The five thumbnails demonstrate the results when different sets of values are applied to the picture – click on the best one and then click the **OK** button to apply the effect.

You can make fine adjustments to the one you choose by clicking on it
and then clicking the **Options...** button to open a second dialog.

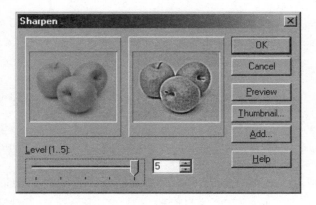

The level can be adjusted by dragging the pointer on the scale or
entering a value of 1 – 5 in the panel alongside.

PhotoHouse, *PerfectPhoto* (below left) and *PhotoEditor* (below right)
have similar, but simpler dialogs which require the user the drag a slider
along a scale until the image is as good as it can get.

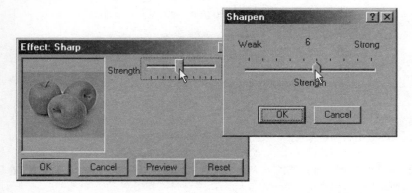

As with most effects, sharpening will be applied to the whole picture or
to a selection. (For more information about selecting, read the section

on page 131.) This means that if only part of a picture needs sharpening, you can select the area and apply the effect to that area only without affecting the rest of the picture.

In addition to the usual 'cover everything' sharpening, some photo applications feature a sharpening effect that can be 'painted on'.

PhotoEditor and *PhotoImpact* feature this effect. In *PhotoImpact*, select the tool from the **Retouch** tool bar which is opened by clicking on the arrow at the bottom right corner.

The tool to select is the dark pyramid, second from right and the mouse pointer inherits the pyramid shape. In *PhotoEditor*, the tool is selected from the button bar.

To use these, simply paint around the areas that require sharpening. As with many of these effects, a graphics tablet is the preferred tool, but acceptable results can be had with a mouse.

Unsharp

If sharpening doesn't give the results you'd hoped for, try Unsharp. The unsharp option is basically a different method of sharpening an image. It works by subtracting an average value from certain pixels.

The Unsharp dialogs in *PhotoImpact* are similar to those for Sharp. To locate the dialog, click on **Effect** on the menubar, go to **Blur & Sharpen** on the drop down menu and choose **Unsharp...** from the sub menu.

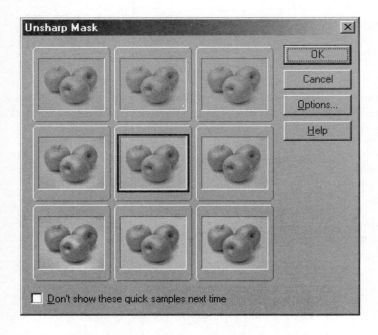

Choose the best example from the nine standard settings provided in the dialog and click the **OK** button to apply the effect. Alternatively you can choose one and then click the **Options...** button to open a second dialog in which you can fine tune the effect.

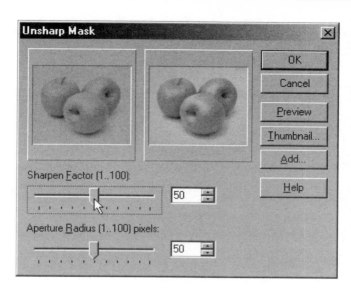

The two sliders allow you to adjust the amount of sharpening and the size of the aperture which will determine the amount of light entering the camera.

PerfectPhoto has a similar but simpler method of applying this effect. The dialog can be found by clicking on **Effects** on the menubar, going to **Effects** on the drop down menu and choosing **Unsharp mask...** from the sub menu.

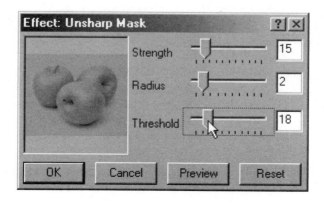

11   Sharpening

PhotoDeluxe has an almost identical dialog which can be found by clicking on **Effects** on the menubar, going to **Sharpen** on the drop down menu and choosing **Unsharp Mask...** from the sub menu.

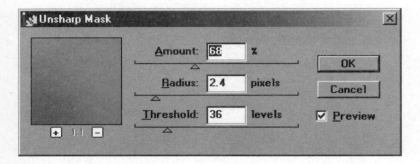

Different pictures will work better than others and you need to experiment. The apples, which was very blurred, responded quite well to unsharp, but not as dramatically as the calculator which can clearly be seen to have improved.

Before, the blur made the numbers on the keys indistinct. After applying unsharp, the legends are much clearer and more easily read.

Blurring & Softening

Out of focus

I've yet to find a digital imaging program that doesn't include the facility to soften or blur a picture. You need to use this effect with great care as the picture can end up looking like it was badly photographed. But with care, this effect can produce some excellent effects.

Soft and romantic

A photograph which is too sharp can look clinical. A softer focus makes a softer and warmer picture.

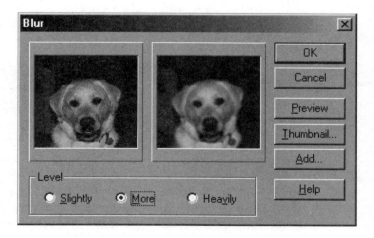

If you're using *PhotoImpact*, the Blur dialog can be found by clicking on **Effects** on the menubar, going to **Blur and Sharpen** on the drop down menu and choosing **Blur**. As can be clearly seen in the thumbnail: a little blurring is good but too much makes the picture look out of focus.

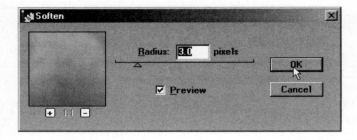

PhotoDeluxe has both Soften and Blur, both of which can be found by clicking on **Effects** on the menubar, going to **Blur** on the drop down menu and choosing either **Blur** or **Soften** from the sub menu. Blur has no control but just adds a small amount of the effect to the image or a selection within the image. If you want to blur it a little more, choose **Blur More** from the sub menu.

To soften a picture, choose **Soften** from the sub menu and the dialog above opens. The **+** and **−** signs on the left adjust the scale of the thumbnail. The main adjustment on this dialog is the amount of softening which is entered as the radius in pixels.

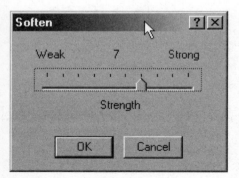

PhotoEditor also refers to this process as softening, and choosing this option opens a simple dialog with a 10 point scale which can be adjusted by dragging the pointer along the scale. This menu can be found by clicking on **Effects** on the menubar and choosing **Soften...** from the drop down menu. Remember, if you don't like what it's done to your picture you can undo the action by entering CTRL Z or discard the picture without saving. The latter will cause you to lose any other effects you applied after the last time you saved.

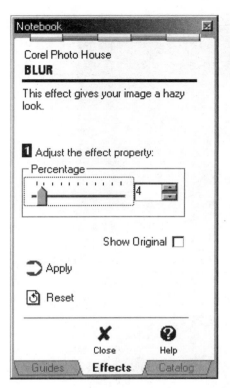

Corel's *PhotoHouse* uses Blur which is operated in a similar way to *PhotoEditor*: drag the slider along the scale until you get the effect as you want it. When you've got it right, click on **Apply** to fix the effect.

Blur is found by clicking on **Effects** on the menubar, going to **Blur Effects** on the drop down menu and choosing **Blur...** from the sub menu. If you're using **Guided Activities**, choose **Prepare Image**, **Effects** and **Blur**. You can apply this effect to either all of the image of a selected area of it.

Clicking on **Effects** on the menubar, going to **Effects** on the drop down and choosing **Blur...** in IBM's *PerfectPhoto*, opens a dialog which offers 6 different types of blur.

Each effect works in a slightly different way and requires noticeably different amounts of **Strength** to achieve the desired effect.

Having softened the image, further effects can then be added like cropping and then blurring or fogging the edge.

This vignette was created in *PerfectPhoto* using the outline blur which is found by clicking on **Selected Area** on the menubar and choosing **Outline Blur...** from the drop down menu.

Making it move

There are a variety of effects you can apply to a picture to give the impression of movement. Most, but not all, involve a degree of blurring, but usually in one direction rather than all over.

This is one of the now almost obligatory effects which every image processing application seems to offer. Some, however, make a better job of it than others.

The motion blur tool can be found in *PerfectPhoto* by clicking on **Effects** on the menubar, going to **Photo** on the drop down menu and choosing **Motion Blur...** on the sub menu.

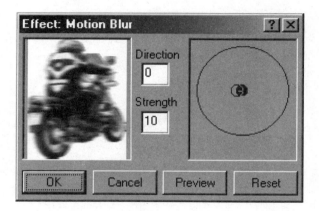

The black circle in the centre of the dialog represents the centre of the picture or the selection.

The small circle can be dragged out to determine the Strength (or length) and Direction of the blur. The Strength setting dictates how long the blur will be: the longer the blur, the faster the object will appear to be moving. Direction can also be entered as a number (of degrees), whilst the number for the Strength setting is the number of pixels which will be affected by the action.

Speed blur (subject)

Blurring the subject gives the impression that the camera was stationary when the picture was taken and a fast moving object passed in front of the lens. The background is clearly sharp and hence stationary, but the blurred bike and rider give the impression of movement.

This effect requires a great deal of experimentation to get a convincing result. In this example, the blurring has been applied to the selected area which was closely cut. It's at the correct angle (about 5° below horizontal), but the strength setting is too low. With the strength doubled, or even trebled, the result is more convincing.

Speed blur (background)

This is a much easier effect to produce. The settings for this blur were exactly the same as the previous example, except the background was blurred, not the bike and rider.

Speed blur (centre)

You can produce a similar effect very easily without the need to closely cut around the object. This is not as good as the previous methods, but will give the impression of speed.

Begin by selecting an area of the picture and softly blurring the inner edges.

Next, put a soft blur onto the selection. This will help disguise the outline of the selected area. Invert the selection and add the motion blur.

The amount of motion blur applied to the background should be only slightly more than the blur applied to the selection.

Whiz lines

Cartoonists frequently use whiz lines to show speed. *PerfectPhoto* has this feature (as does *PhotoImpact*) although it's referred to as wind.

Like most effects, whiz lines can be applied to a small section of the picture, or all of it. For this effect, you don't need to cut very close to the subject.

Once you've selected the area you want to add whiz lines to, click on **Effects** on the menubar, go to **Photo** on the drop down menu and choose **Wind...** from the sub menu.

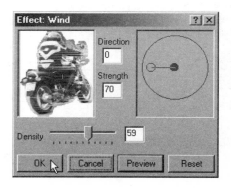

The dialog allows you to determine the density of the lines (how many of them there are), the direction (which is decided by dragging the small circle) and the strength (how long they are). Clicking OK fixes the whiz lines onto the selected part of the picture.

Circular motion

No picture of a moving wheeled vehicle is going to look convincing if the wheels are not turning.

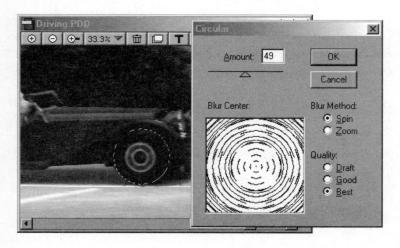

PhotoDeluxe has a useful feature in the sub menu which can be found by clicking on **Effects** on the menubar and choosing **Blur** from the drop down menu. Circular Blur will make a stationary wheel look like it's revolving. Choose the Oval Selection Tool from the Selection dialog and select one of the wheels. Open the Circular Blur dialog and choose **Spin**. The amount of spin can be adjusted by clicking and dragging the slider or entering a number into the **Amount:** box.

The main part of this picture (Biffer in the car) is described in the section on Layers on page 177. After the wheels were blurred to show rotation, the car was given a slight motion blur (using *PhotoDeluxe*) and placed on the background which was given quite a strong motion blur. The picture was then placed in *PhotoHouse* where Biffer's head was selected and wind lines added.

Zoom blur

This clever feature found in *PhotoDeluxe* blurs a picture in a way that
makes it look as though you're rushing into the picture. To access the
dialog click on **Effects** on the menubar, go to **Blur** of the drop down
menu and choose **Circular**. When the dialog opens, select **Zoom**.

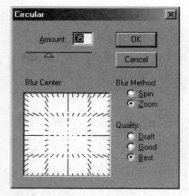

At first glance one might be forgiven
for thinking that there are only two
settings to be dealt with: the **Quality**
of the blur and the **Amount** of blur.
In fact there is a third adjustment and
this is pinpointing the centre of the
blur and this is achieved by dragging
the diagram in the box entitled **Blur
Centre:**.

For most pictures, a value of 35 is quite sufficient to achieve a good
effect.

Pixelating & Mosaics

An undesirable effect?

The type of picture taken with a digital camera or scanner is known as a bitmap image. Each dot or pixel is given its own colour and the picture is saved as a series of numbers relating to each pixel. If you try enlarging a bitmap image you'll see that each of the dots gets enlarged and as the picture is made bigger, it's possible to see the dots as clearly defined squares.

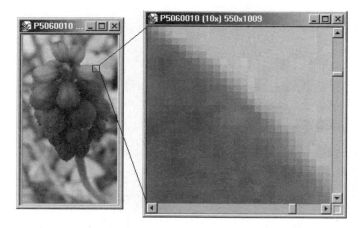

The image above shows a small section of a picture which has been blown up to the point where the pixels can be easily seen. The picture on the right is 10 times larger, but this effect happens as soon as you scale a picture above full size or 1:1. We usually try to eliminate pixelation, as it is known, but a similar effect can create some interesting pictures.

Pixelated images are frequently used on TV news programmes when reporting on someone whose identity must be kept secret. In this case a small area of a picture (usually the face) is pixelated to protect the innocent (or the guilty).

Most imaging software offers this facility, which is usually referred to as Mosaic, and in most cases can be applied to the whole picture or to a small portion.

Strictly speaking, this is not the same as pixelation but to the untrained eye it might be mistaken for it. Mosaic works by taking groups of pixels and averaging them so that they are all the same colour. The more pixels used to create the cells, the 'chunkier' the mosaic will be.

You need to use this effect with care because an image which is totally mosaicked can look as though it's simply a poorly shot picture and that it's just been enlarged too much.

Many programs offer a range of variations on this theme. *PhotoDeluxe* has six options including the standard Mosaic which may be found by clicking on **Effects** on the menubar, going to **Pixelate** on the drop down menu and choosing the required effect from the sub menu. With the exception of **Facet** and **Fragment**, each option leads to a dialog where you can choose details like the size of the cells which can be entered either as a number or chosen by dragging the slider.

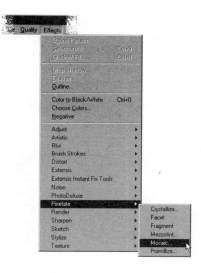

The thumbnail picture on the left of the dialog can be scaled to show what the picture will look like at different scales.

With the correct subject you can get some interesting effects, but there are lots of variations on the theme of removing detail from photos.

PhotoDeluxe has an effect which they call Crystalise. Like Mosaic, it averages groups of pixels to form cells of uniform colour. Unlike Mosaic which generates square cells, Crystalise generates cells rather like crystals of random shape with four or five sides.

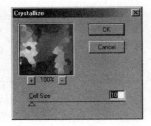

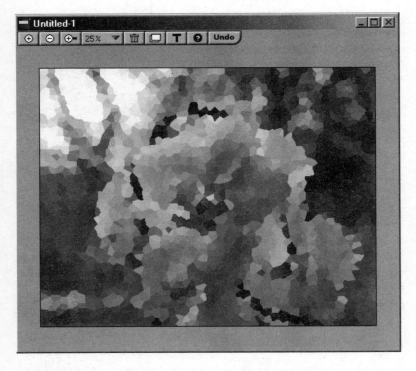

The trick with this effect is to get the size of the crystals correct for the photograph you are using. You should aim to get them large enough to be able to see the effect, but not too large so you make the picture unrecognisable. In the picture above, it's virtually impossible to determine the subject because the crystals are too large.

PhotoHouse also has some similar effects which can be accessed by clicking on **Effects** on the menubar, going to **Artistic Effects** on the drop down menu and choosing **Crystalise** from the sub menu. Crystalise is different from the effects of the same name found in *PhotoDeluxe* which includes one that looks as though you're viewing the subject through glass of the type that's often fitted in bathroom windows.

When you've selected the required effect from the menus, the options may be found in the **Guided Activities** panel on the left of the window. You can choose one of four basic effects with a choice of either tiling that effect over the picture or stretching it to fit the picture. (The latter produces a distortion effect rather than a pixelating effect.)

The slider can be dragged across the scale to alter the size of the cells being used to create the pattern.

If a section of the picture has been selected then the effect will be applied to that area only.

Under a different heading in *PhotoHouse* is **Tile** which gives the effect that the picture has been built up from a number of printed tiles and laid on a floor by a tiler who really isn't very good. You can choose to leave the gaps as the background colour (as is the case here) or

have them filled with bits of the image. Either way, if the tiles on my kitchen floor were laid like this, I'd want a refund.

To get to this effect, click on **Effects** on the menubar, go down to **Cool & Fun Effects** on the drop down menu and choose **Puzzle** from the sub menu.

Exactly the same effect can be found in *PerfectPhoto*, which also features Mosaic and Scatter where pixels are moved around to give the effect of viewing the image through frosted glass.

All of these effects in *PerfectPhoto* can be found by clicking on **Effects**

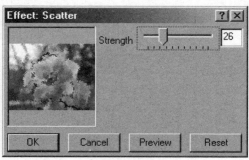

on the menubar, going to **Effects** on the drop down menu and choosing **Tile...**, **Mosaic...** or **Scatter...** from the sub menu. They all lead to a dialog in which you enter the strength of the effect.

In the case of Tile, you can also choose the amount each 'tile' is offset and in the case of Mosaic, the way the picture is illuminated.

Like many of the features in *PhotoImpact*, choosing an effect leads to a dialog which offers nine variations of the effect. Clicking on the desired level of the effect applies it to your picture, but you can also click the **Options...** button to create your own settings.

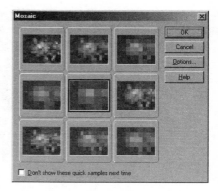

PhotoImpact features the mosaic effect but also has a variation called Facet. To access this effect, click on **Effects** on the menubar, go to **Camera Lens** on the drop down menu and choose **Facet...** from the sub menu.

Another crystalised effect can be found in *PhotoEditor*. Click on **Effects** on the menubar and choose **Stained Glass...** from the drop down menu. This opens a dialog in which several options are available.

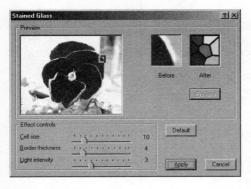

The top slider allows you to adjust the size of the cells. As with all of these effects, you must spend time getting the cells the right size, but it's easier with this effect because you can see the effect almost regardless of how small you make the cells. Each cell is bordered by a line which represents the lead in a stained glass window, and the thickness of the line can be adjusted using the middle slider. The bottom slider is used to adjust the intensity of light and can give the effect of a stained glass window with the sun coming through.

Clicking on the **Preview** button shows what the effect will be like in the square area on the thumbnail view. The square can be dragged around to show what the effect will be like in any area of the picture.

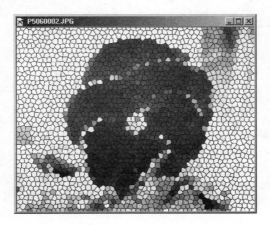

PhotoFX2 by Greenstreet Technology offers a huge range of pixelating effects including Mosaic, but these can only be applied to the whole picture and not a selected area of the picture.

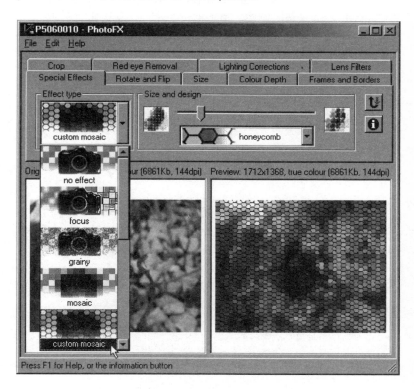

By clicking on the **Effect type** button, a drop down menu displays a variety of effects including **Custom Effect**. If this option is chosen a second drop down menu can be accessed from which you can choose the particular custom effect you require. The slider above can be dragged side to side to make a finer or coarser pattern.

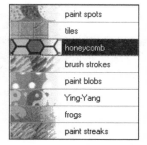

Pixelating the background

You can achieve some interesting effects by pixelating part of the picture. On page 122 is a picture with part of the foreground pixelated, but applying the effect to the background will have a similar effect to blurring the background: it make the subject stand out by reducing distractions behind.

Having removed Biffer from the picture, the background was pixelated using *PerfectPhoto*. The result keeps the original background (which means that you don't have to be very precise when removing it), but it doesn't distract from the subject.

Removing sections of a picture is discussed on page 131.

Selecting & Cutting

Electronic scissors

Many effects which can be applied to digital pictures requires that an area or areas are marked out enabling an effect to be carried out on a section of the picture rather than the whole picture. It's really rather like taking a printed picture and cutting a section out with a pair of scissors.

Predefined shapes

All of the five featured applications have a variety of tools for making a selection. One that is common to all is a simple rectangular selection tool.

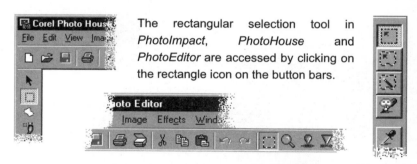

The rectangular selection tool in *PhotoImpact*, *PhotoHouse* and *PhotoEditor* are accessed by clicking on the rectangle icon on the button bars.

The selection is made by dragging from any corner to the diagonally opposite corner (eg top left to bottom right). *PhotoEditor* benefits from having adjusting nodes so that small alterations can be made to the size of the selected area by dragging the nodes.

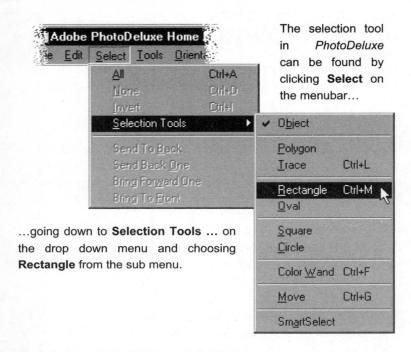

The selection tool in *PhotoDeluxe* can be found by clicking **Select** on the menubar…

…going down to **Selection Tools …** on the drop down menu and choosing **Rectangle** from the sub menu.

In *PerfectPhoto*, the rectangular selection tool can be found in the **Tools** floating window.

As with *PhotoImpact*, *PhotoHouse* and *PhotoEditor*, the rectangular selection is made by dragging between two diagonally opposite corners. If a mistake is made, drag again and the second selection will supersede the first one.

Both *PerfectPhoto* and *PhotoDeluxe* also offer additional shapes which can be used to select an area, but they are applied in the same way as the basic rectangle selection tool: drag over diagonally opposite corners. The point to note with the **Square** and **Circle** selection tools in *PhotoDeluxe* is that you can *only* get a perfect square or a perfect circle. If the shape you want is not perfectly square or circular, you'll need to choose **Rectangle** or **Oval**.

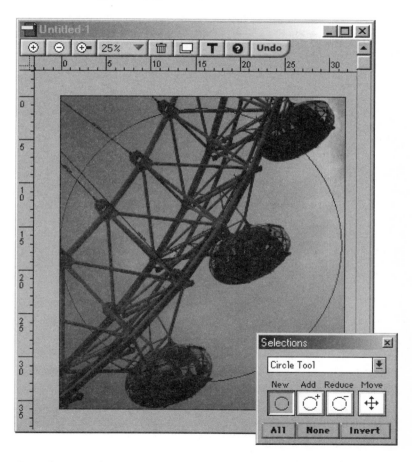

PhotoDeluxe's Circle selection tool gives a perfect circle.

Freehand selection

For the beginner, selecting a regular area is likely to be the most frequently used selection process, but for more advanced work it may be preferable to capture an irregular area. Hand drawing to select an irregular area is one way of achieving this and all tasks of this nature are best carried out with a graphics tablet if you have one.

The simplest version is the freehand tool found in *PhotoHouse* and is selected from the toolbar on the left. When you move the mouse pointer into the picture it changes from the usual arrow to a cross with a piece of rope. Move to the edge of the area you wish to select, press and hold the left mouse button and whilst holding it, drag around the area you wish to select.

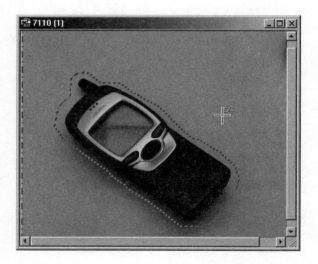

When the mouse button is released, the area will be joined to form a continuous loop. Further areas may also be selected.

This is a simple tool to use and it may be made easier by enlarging the picture, providing all the area you wish to select is visible.

PhotoDeluxe has a similar freehand tool called Trace which can be selected by clicking on **Select** on the menubar, going to **Selection**

Tools on the drop down menu and choosing **Trace** from the sub menu. Both of these tools are very approximate and can't really be used to get tight into the area you want to select.

If you want more accuracy, use Smart Select in *PhotoDeluxe* which may be found by going through the same menus as before but choosing **SmartSelect** at the bottom of the sub menu.

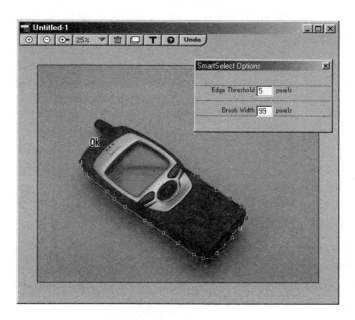

Smart Select takes a little bit of practice to get really good, but it's worth persevering. All you need to do is click on the edge of the area you wish to select and then trace the pointer around the edge of the area. The software will automatically adjust the selection line so that it is as close as possible to the object you're trying to select. When you want to finish, double click the left mouse button.

When you choose Smart Select a small dialog pops up into which you can enter two values. **Edge Threshold** determines how sensitive the tool is to colour differences. The lower the value, the less sensitive it is, meaning that the selection line will lock itself onto areas of high contrast.

Brush Width determines how far the mouse pointer can be away from the area you're trying to select. The larger the number, the less accurate you need to be with the mouse or graphic tablet pen.

This tool is especially useful when you want to select an object like the phone which is very dark and on a light background. A value of 5 for Edge Threshold and 99 for Brush Width meant that I could trace the phone very accurately in a few seconds. Each picture will require different settings and it may take several attempts to get the settings right for a particular picture.

PhotoDeluxe has a third selection tool called Polygon, which also appears in *PerfectPhoto* as the cutter tool which is found in the toolbox.

When selected and the mouse is moved into the picture, the pointer becomes a cutter.

For this exercise it's often best to enlarge the picture, not by so much that you can no longer see what the picture is, but by two or three times is usually enough. If the whole of the area you wish to select is not visible it's not a problem, as the picture will automatically scroll when you get near to the edge of the window.

To mark an area, click the left mouse button at some point on the edge of the area you wish to select, move the mouse a short distance and click again. Continue moving, clicking as you go until you have navigated around the area. Double click to finish.

The area will have been marked out by a series of connected straight lines.

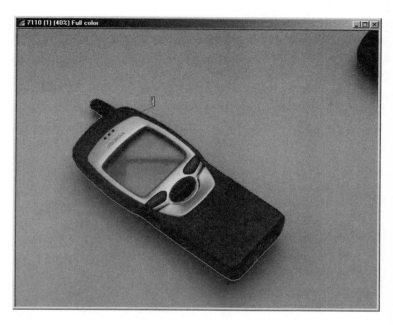

If you enlarged the view enough and used sufficiently short lines to navigate around corners, the final result should look perfect when viewed full size.

With both the polygon tool in *PhotoDeluxe* and *PerfectPhoto*'s cutter, try to set the line on the outside of the area you're trying to select rather than inside. You can always remove the surplus area later but it's harder to add bits that you accidentally let fall outside the selected area.

Another useful freehand selection tool that's worth learning how to use can be found in *PhotoHouse*. The brush selection tool allows you to 'paint' over the area you wish to select. The tool is chosen from the button bar on the left of the window and when selected, additional settings are provided in the Guided Activities panel.

The size and shape of the brush can be selected and your choice should be determined by the shape of the area you wish to select. If the area you are trying to select has lots of corners, you'll need a brush shape with a corner, whereas if you are trying to mark out an area like the Nokia phone which has no corners, you'll need to choose a round brush. You may need to use more than one brush to select a given area.

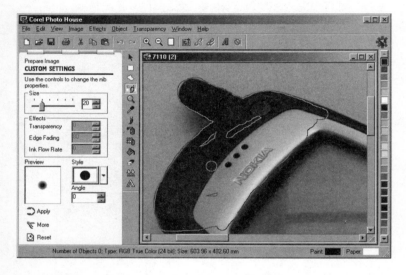

When the correct brush size and shape has been chosen the pointer is moved into the picture where it will inherit the brush shape. Each time the mouse button is pressed (or the pen is pressed onto the graphics tablet) the brush becomes active and area begins to be 'painted'. The mouse or pen should be moved back and forth as if you are painting with a brush.

You'll need to be careful when painting up to an edge and you might find that a change of paint brush will be helpful. The larger brushes will fill in large areas quickly, while the smaller brushes will be needed for 'cutting-in' – a painter's term for taking paint close to an edge without going over – when painting a window frame without getting paint on the glass, for example.

This is one of the occasions when a mouse is not the best tool to use. You can get fairly good results with a standard (but good quality) mouse, but a graphics tablet will give much better results, as painting with a paint-brush like tool is more natural.

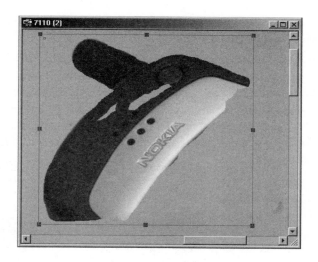

Compare the selection from the previous picture with the area shown above. The two light areas near the on/off button were not painted and are shown in the background colour. It's unlikely you'd really leave an area this size, but small dots are very easy to leave. You'll also notice that the area just below the maker's name has not been very carefully followed.

These errors are both easily made, and improvement in your technique comes with practice. In fact, practice is required before any of these tools can be mastered. What also comes with practice is knowing which selection tool to use in which situation. There are no hard and fast rules – you'll eventually find the ones that suit you best.

Colour detection

There are several automated selection tools and whilst these might seem to be the universal solution to all selection problems, they are not and you'll frequently find that you'll sometimes need to revert to some of the manual selection tools previously described. These tools are really invaluable when the subject is so complicated that drawing around it would be impossible. The London Eye, for example, is a mass of beams and cables. Selecting the ironwork or the background to separate them would be extremely time consuming, if not impossible.

Two of the automatic selection tools (*PhotoImpact* and *PerfectPhoto*) work in much the same way: once the tool is chosen you need to set a level which will determine how accurately an area will be traced. A low value means it's very sensitive to colour change and only a small area will be outlined, whereas a higher value will disregard slight variations in colour enabling a much larger area to be outlined and consequently selected.

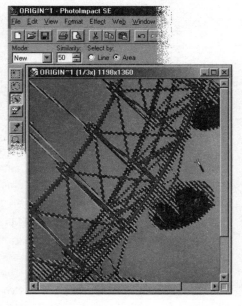

PhotoImpact's Magic Wand can be chosen from the vertical button bar on the left and the value box (labelled **Similarity**) will appear just below the menubar.

In the illustration on the right, the value has been set to 50 which is midway in the range. Clicking on one of the beams has selected the whole of the structure except for a couple of small areas on the capsules which are mainly glass and a totally different colour from the rest of the structure.

A slightly higher value will select the rest of the capsule, but as parts of the capsule are similar to the background, parts of the sky may also find their way into the selection

PerfectPhoto's Magic Wand can be found on the toolbox and at the bottom of the toolbox is the Range setting. As with *PhotoImpact*, the range is 1 to 100, but 50 is usually a good starting point.

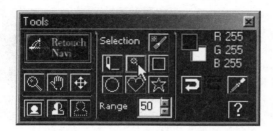

Clicking anywhere on the picture will select an area bounded by pixels that are sufficiently different from that which was clicked on. How different, is determined by the value entered into **Range**.

Clicking on part of the background will accurately select it (as shown here), but clicking on part of the London Eye will select that.

The ColourWand tool in *PhotoDeluxe* is found by clicking **Select** on the menubar, going to **Selection Tools** on the drop down menu and choosing **Colour Wand** from the sub menu. This works in a slightly different way in that there is no value to enter. Instead, you are allowed to make

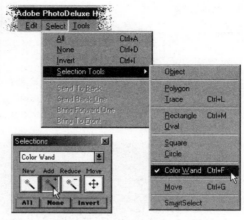

multiple selections: each time you click the mouse button, the area selected can be added to the current selection provided the **Add** button is clicked in the **Selections** toolbox.

One click on the ironwork and most is selected. A second click on another beam will select some more and a third click on the capsule selects the rest.

Inverting the selection

After selecting an area, most applications offer several options, including **Invert**. Inverting a selection is a useful tool to know about because it can save a great deal of time. If you wanted to select all of the sky surrounding the London Eye picture, rather than clicking on every piece of sky that appears between every beam and cable, it is much easier to select the London Eye and then invert the selection.

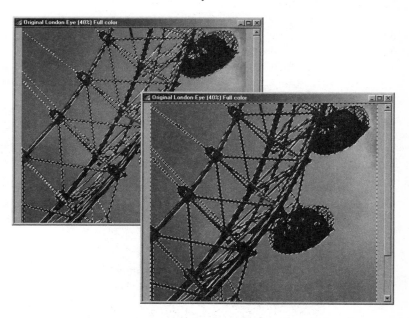

Same picture, same selection, but the lower picture has had the selection inverted. Look closely at the top right corner. The dotted line clearly shows the sky, up to the edge of the picture, is the selection.

Removing the selection

If you want to deselect an area previously selected, in most cases clicking the right hand mouse button whilst the mouse pointer is in the window containing the picture will open a menu. One of the entries might be **Remove selection**, **Cancel Selection** or just **None** and choosing this will cancel the selection. In some cases, a separate toolbox will contain a button which will undo a selection.

Adjusting a selection

Making an irregular selection is not always as precise as one would like and almost inevitably, whichever tool was used to mark a selection, some parts of what you wanted to select will have been missed, and some parts you didn't want selected will have been included.

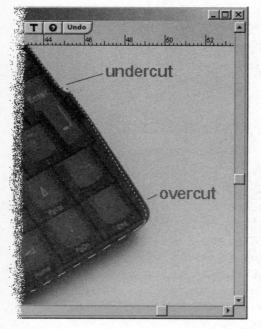

The picture clearly shows the problem: one part of the selection has been undercut (meaning that some of the background has been included in the selection) whilst the lower right corner has been over-cut (meaning that part of the intended selection hasn't been included).

Many applications (including *PhotoDeluxe* (see dialog above) and *PhotoImpact*) offer the facility to add to selections and subtract from them. In the example shown in the picture, select **Add** and re-mark the lower left corner of the selection and it will be added to the existing selection. Similarly, choose **Reduce** and mark the area of background that has been included in the selection to remove it.

Cropping a Picture

Cutting down to size

This is one of the simplest processes, yet is not always implemented as well as it could be. But even at its worse, cropping a digital picture is a great deal easier than getting out a knife and ruler and trying to crop a printed photo, if for no other reason than, if you get is wrong, you can have another go with the digital snap! If you cut the top from someone's head on a printed photograph, that's how it will stay.

All applications work in much the same way: drag a rectangular box over the area of the photo you want to keep and then choose **Crop** from either the menu or the toolbar. (More information about selecting part of an image can be found in the section on Selecting on page 131.)

Having selected an area in *PhotoImpact*, choosing **Crop** from the menu removes everything except the contents of the selected area. As always, *PhotoImpact* automatically re-scales the picture so that it is as large as possible within the area of the window.

Note the difference between **Crop** and **Cut**. The latter removes the current selection. However many digital imaging applications will allow you to invert the selection, so the un-selected area becomes the selected area. You can then Cut and it will remove the area currently regarded as the selection. In short, **Invert** followed by **Cut** is the same as **Crop**.

PhotoEditor considerately provides nodes on the marked area so that you can finely adjust the size of the selected area before cropping. Simply move the mouse pointer onto one of the nodes and drag in or out. The corner nodes adjust both the length and the height, whilst the nodes at the centre of the sides adjust only the width or height.

Select by size

If you want to crop an area to an exact size, Microsoft's *PhotoEditor* is the application to choose. You will need to spend some time calculating the sizes you want if you're going to use this tool. To get to this dialog, click on **Image** on the menubar and choose **Crop...** from the drop down menu.

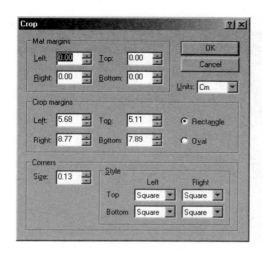

It's best to begin deciding what units you want to use – centimetres, inches or pixels. You can select either a rectangle or ellipse (oval) with this tool and you then need to decide where the left edge of the selection should be relative to the margin. The right, top and bottom edges are calculated next. Finally, if you wish, you can choose rounded corners, and decide on the radius. The Mat dialogs help you position the image on the 'paper' by setting the distance between the edge of the picture and the edge of the 'paper'.

Overhangs

A popular and effective trick is to crop a picture, but leaving a section hanging outside the natural edge. This effect emphasises the subject and brings it out of the page, producing an almost 3D effect.

There are two ways of doing this, but the easiest is using a program that will allow you to add to your selection. *PhotoDeluxe* is one such program.

Open the image you wish to work with, then open the **Selections** toolbox which can be found by clicking on **View** on the menubar and choosing **Show Selections** from the drop down menu. Choose the rectangle tool and mark the area you wish to select.

Ensure **Add** is clicked on the **Selections** toolbox, and choose the **Polygon** selection tool. It's also worth enlarging the picture so that you can see exactly what you're doing. You need to begin marking around the overhang beginning at the exact point where the rectangle selection crosses the part of the photo that is to overhang. In the case of this Alstroemeria, the freehand selection begins where the top of the leaf on the right intersects the dotted line which is the original rectangular selection. Double click the left mouse button when you've navigated around the overhanging object and you are exactly over the second intersection between the over-hanging part of the drawing and the line of the rectangular selection.

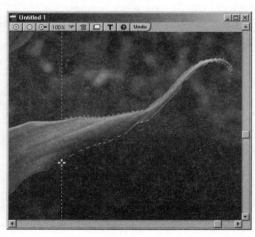

If **Add** is chosen, the freehand selection will be added to the current selection and become part of it.

Do the same with any other parts you wish to overhang and crop the image.

If you don't have *PhotoDeluxe* or an application which can add to selections, you can still create this effect, although it will take a little more effort.

Select the rectangular area as before and cut it. (Read the section on Cutting, Copying and Pasting on page 155.)

Create a new document which is the same size as the picture you're working with and paste the cut section into the blank document. (This process is outlined in the Loading and Saving section on page 25.)

Return to the original document which now has a piece missing from it which you previously removed. Using a freehand selection tool like *PerfectPhoto*'s cutter, mark around the section you which to overhang very carefully.

The area which is adjacent to the area previously removed must be marked very accurately so that it matches the main part of the picture. (It you do not select close enough to the edge, you'll get a white line between the overhanging part and the main part of the photograph. If you go too far you'll lose some of the overhanging part and it won't match correctly.)

When you've selected it, cut it and paste it into the new document, and carefully drag the selection into position.

Who said photos have to be square?

Square or rectangular photos are the most common but that's only because most photos are commercially printed and rectangular pictures produce less waste.

Some photo editing applications allow you to crop pictures to an ellipse (or oval), circle and even stars and hearts.

Irregular pictures

You can get some interesting effects by cropping a picture into an irregular shape.

Most photo editing applications can create irregular selections, although rarely do you see it used in this context. I used *PerfectPhoto* for this job. The tool to use is the cutter which can be used as a freehand tool or as a tool to draw a series of straight lines to mark out a selected area.

Carefully mark around the areas and crop.

You can use this process to emphasise lines which naturally occur in the picture. For example, if you have a picture of someone who is leaning, you can draw a selection line to emphasise the fact. With care you can mate this picture to another picture which has been cut at a similar angle.

If you don't get the angles cut absolutely perfectly, careful positioning (one on top of another) can hide any slight error. If all else fails, you can either use an edge fade between the pictures or draw lines between them as shown on the previous page.

This is rather like a collage produced electronically. Pictures can be very roughly cut up and pasted onto a new blank document.

Origami

The ancient art of paper folding gets a new lease of life if the paper has been personalised with some photographs. If you want to practise your cropping skills, try making one of the charming trinket boxes.

Assuming that your printer will accept nothing larger than A4 paper, and it prints about 2-3mm from the edges of the paper, the largest box of this design you'll be able to fold is about 6.5cm x 3.3cm deep.

To make this trinket box you'll need to prepare four pictures cropped to 6.5cm x 3.3cm and rotated by 45°.

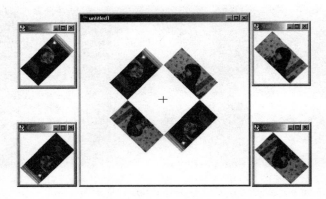

Create a document 20cm square and arrange the four pictures in the centre to form a diamond. Marking a cross in the centre will help you position them. (Refer to the section on copying and pasting on page 155.) It's important to get them positioned accurately. A line drawn across the bottom of the picture will also help you cut the paper later

Next, print out the picture on some 140g/m^2 paper. This weight seems to be the best for this project. The lighter 80g/m^2 is too flimsy, whilst thicker card is difficult to fold.

After printing, allow it to dry thoroughly; preferably overnight. The first job is to make the paper square and the mark at the centre should help.

Next, fold along the outside edges of each picture. You may prefer to score the lines first. To do this use a steel rule (not a wooden or plastic rule) and a knife which isn't too sharp. Cut lightly into the card, but not so hard that you cut right

through. Turn the folded sheet over and fold along the lines at the bottom of each picture. Fold the two opposite edges, open up the fold and then fold the other two edges.

You'll need to make the folds very accurately otherwise the finished box will be a little uneven. Open the last two folds you made and check that the folds are even. You can sometimes make adjustments by re-folding.

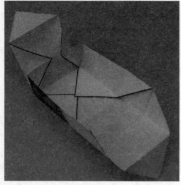

On the back will now be four triangular tabs which have a fold from the last process. This fold needs to be folded the other way.

Next, place the box on its base and fold up two opposite sides. When you lift one of the ends, the corners should form themselves into triangular tucks which can be seen at the top of the picture (left). These tucks need to be pressed flat so that when the face is folded over the side with the photograph, it lays flat. The triangular flap at the very top of the picture should lay flat on the bottom of the box. When one end is complete, turn it around and fold the other end to match the first.

Although not authentic practice, a dab of glue on the triangular flap will help keep it all together. If you wish, a piece of card about 6cm square will also help strengthen the bottom of the box.

Remarkably, if this box is made correctly, it is watertight, although I'm not quite sure what one might do with a box capable of holding an egg-cup full of water.

Cut, Copy & Paste

Transferring data

Most applications support cutting, copying and pasting and these functions can usually be found by clicking on **Edit** on the menubar and choosing the required action from the drop down menu.

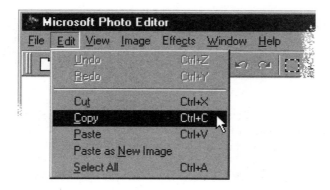

These actions can be used to move or copy pictures or an area of a picture between different documents within an application and, within certain limitations, to move or copy between documents in different applications.

It's important to know how these work and the differences between them but to fully understand this section, you should refer to the section on Selecting an Area on page 131.

Clipboard

The clipboard is an area of the computer's main memory which can temporarily store data. The data may be (for example) a piece of text, a piece of a picture or a whole picture. You can view the contents of the clipboard using the Clipboard Viewer which is one of the applications installed as part of *Windows95/98/ME*.

Running the *Clipboard Viewer* 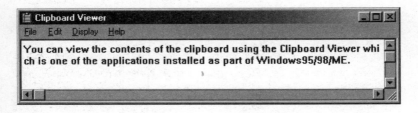 application opens a window which displays the current contents of the clipboard.

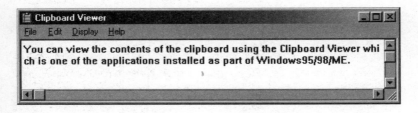

> **Cut**. This command removes the picture or part of the picture from the current location and stores it in the clipboard. Anything previously in the clipboard will be overwritten and consequently lost.
>
> **Copy**. This command is identical to Cut except that the original remains in place.
>
> **Paste**. This will copy the contents of the clipboard into the currently active document (the one with the blue bar at the top of the document window) provided the application can support data of that type. You can use this command as many times as you like.

Shortcuts

Almost every application, whether it be a text based application like a word processor or an application that is designed to handle pictures, has the same keyboard shortcuts for the three basic editing functions:

CRTL X	Cut
CTRL C	Copy
CTRL V	Paste

Limitations

All applications support these actions when the picture or part of a picture is cut, copied and pasted between documents within the same application. For example, if you are using *PhotoEditor* and have two documents open, you can cut or copy either the whole picture or a section of the picture between documents.

These two documents were both opened in Microsoft's PhotoEditor. An area has been marked (shown by the dotted line in the left picture) and copied. The mouse was clicked in the right picture so that that document became the active one, and the selection was pasted.

You can cut, copy a rectangular section of a picture in one application and paste it into another picture in virtually any other application.

Where the system becomes a little uncertain is when you copy a part of a picture which has been opened in one application and try to paste it into a picture in another different application. If the part or section of the picture you're copying has effects or features which are peculiar to that particular application (ie the application you are copying from) then it might not work as you expect.

In this example, the picture on the left was opened in PerfectPhoto and an irregular selection was marked and copied. (Again, you can see the selection marked by the dotted line.) When it was pasted into a document in PhotoEditor it inherited the area surrounding the original irregular shape and became a rectangle.

The other feature that frequently won't copy between applications is a transparent area. When it arrives in the second application you may well find it's lost its transparency.

Paste as New

A useful feature found in many photo imaging applications **is Paste as New**. This places the current contents of the clipboard into a new document. If this is done within the same application then any special qualities (irregular selection, transparent areas) will be maintained.

Resizing & Resolution

Properties

If you right click on a file icon in a filer window, a menu pops up and clicking on the bottom entry opens the **Property** dialog for that file.

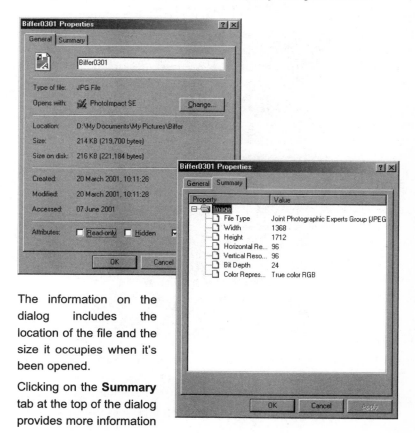

The information on the dialog includes the location of the file and the size it occupies when it's been opened.

Clicking on the **Summary** tab at the top of the dialog provides more information about the file. If it's a graphic file the information includes its size in pixels and the resolution in pixels per inch (ppi). If you divide the horizontal resolution into the number of pixels in the width, and the vertical resolution into the picture height you'll get the size of the picture in inches.

In the example on the previous page, 1368 horizontal pixels divided by 96 horizontal ppi gives 14¼", whilst 1712 vertical pixels divided by 96 gives about 17¾".

When the file is opened in an application and a ruler is placed on the picture, we can see that this calculation is correct.

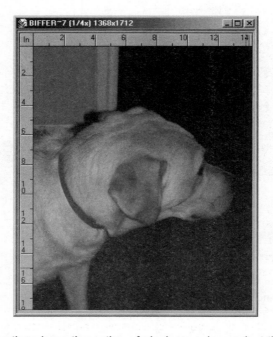

Most applications have the option of placing a ruler against the picture. This picture was opened in *PhotoImpact* and the ruler is selected by clicking on **View** on the menubar and choosing **Ruler** from the drop down menu. The units (inches, centimetres or pixels) can be selected by clicking the ruler icon at the bottom right of the *PhotoImpact* window.

Changing the picture size

Cropping a picture will reduce the size but will remove some of the picture. If you want to increase or reduce the size of a picture whilst keeping all of the picture you must alter the dimensions. In *PhotoImpact* the **Dimensions** dialog can be found by clicking **Format** on the menubar and choosing **Dimensions...** from the drop down menu.

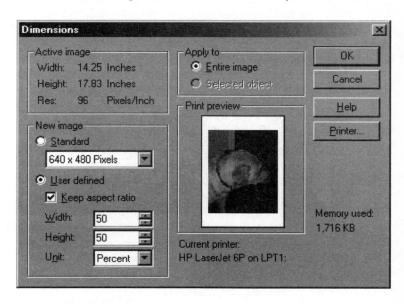

The size of the picture can be altered by either entering a percentage or by altering the physical size. To change the measurement unit, click on the menu arrow alongside **Unit:** and choose the required unit (pixels, inches or centimetres) from the menu.

Remember, if you reduce a picture by 50%, it becomes one quarter of its original area because the percentage reduction refers to each side. So, if a picture is 8" x 4", (32 square inches) reducing by 50% will make the picture 4" x 2" or 8 square inches – one quarter of its original 32 square inches and occupying a quarter of the original file and memory space. The same applies when you're increasing the size which can result in an enormous file both in terms of physical dimensions and the amount of memory it occupies.

PhotoHouse allows you to resize a picture as it is opened. Click on **File** on the menubar and choose **Open...** from the drop down menu. This will open the **Notebook** or **Guided Activities**. Click the **Advanced** button at the bottom which will open the Advanced Open File dialog from which you locate and click the file you wish to open. Choose **Resample** from the menu on the dialog and click the **Open** button.

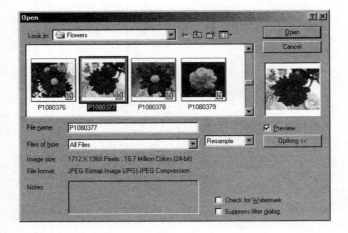

The Resample Image dialog will open and you enter the size you want the picture to be. The current size is given in the top right of the dialog and can be changed by changing either the sizes or entering a percentage of the size. A number greater than 100% will increase the size.

You can work in either inches, pixels or centimetres by choosing from the menu alongside **Units:**, but if you want the picture to remain the same proportion, ensure the **Maintain Aspect Ratio** box is ticked.

Changing the canvas size

You may want to keep the picture the same size and increase the area around it, but surprisingly this is not always supported in photo imaging software. The way to overcome this is to create a new document the size you want and cut and copy the image into it.

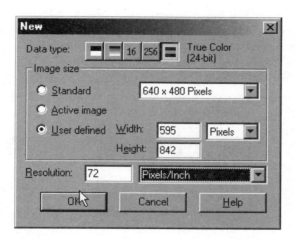

Set the size of the new document in either pixels, inches or centimetres and set the resolution the same as the original picture. Click the **OK** button to create the new document.

Click the right button in the old image to open a menu and choose **All** to select the entire image. Copy the image into the clipboard and paste it into the new blank document. For more information about copy and paste, read the section on page 155.

Changing resolution

The resolution is the number of pixels in a given distance. When creating a new file for display only, there is no point assigning a resolution greater than the display can handle. When printing, on the other hand, you may wish to assign a higher resolution.

Changing the resolution of an existing file will not alter the amount of memory it uses, but will alter its physical dimensions. For example, a file with a resolution of 72 ppi will halve in size if the resolution is increased to 144 ppi. The reason is that you would be cramming twice as many pixels into the same space. So, a 72 ppi picture which is 2" long would contain 144 pixels in total across its length. Increasing the resolution to 144 ppi would put all of those pixels into 1".

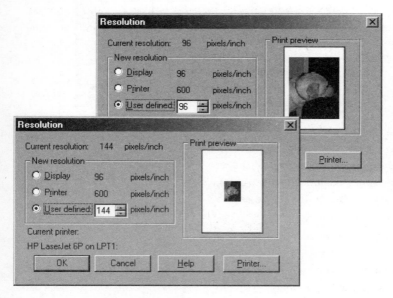

The print previews on the dialogs show the difference. Double the resolution means the picture will halve in size and will not use any less memory.

The printer resolution is determined by the currently assigned printer.

Borders & Vignettes

Wrapping it up

A frame or border can enhance a picture and make the subject stand out, but it needs to be chosen carefully. An ill-considered frame or border can detract from the picture.

Borders

Virtually all digital imaging software provides a facility to create an edge on a picture. Some are very sophisticated and can produce some stunning effects. But even *Paint*, which is supplied with Windows, can be used to produce some interesting effects.

The main problem you'll have when using *Paint* is that you can't reduce the scale of the picture so you might find you're doing a lot of scrolling as you may not be able to see all of the image on screen.

Once you've opened your picture in *Paint*, choose a solid colour and paint four narrow rectangles around the edge of the picture to produce a solid colour border around the picture. You'll have to judge the distances as there is no easy way of measuring unless you increase the scale and choose to have a grid displayed.

Border drawn with white rectangles

Once you've got a plain border around the picture you can add some lines to it.

Simple thick and thin lines can work wonders. Here, a 3-pixel wide black line has been placed 2 pixels away from a 1-pixel black line.

You can make the picture stand out from a plain border or look as though it's been inset simply by adding dark and light lines.

Dark lines at the top and light lines at the bottom make the picture look inset, whilst the reverse makes it stand out.

PerfectPhoto has a border function which will put a border of any colour around your picture, but instead of the hard edged border created in *Paint*, this effect will fade the border into the picture.

The dialog can be found by clicking on **Effects** on the menubar, going to **Effects** on the drop down menu and choosing **Border...** from the sub menu.

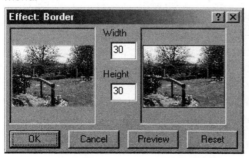

The dialog will work on the whole picture or a selected area. Before entering this dialog, choose the colour from the colour picker which can be found in the Tools dialog.

Using a selection

Most of these effects work on a selected area as well as the whole image. One particularly effective trick is to turn part of the area into greyscale and leave the rest in colour.

The centre section is be in full colour, whilst the outside would be in greyscale. As it's not possible to reproduce this effect in a book printed in black and white, the frame has been put into negative.

You can do this in most digital imaging applications. Choose the rectangular selection tool, draw a section in the centre of the picture and then reverse or invert the selection. (Inverting deselects the current selection and selects the currently unselected area.) In this situation, the frame around the centre rectangle becomes the selection and choosing negative, greyscale or almost any other effect will apply it to the frame whilst leaving the centre of the picture untouched.

Although this effect was carried out using a rectangle to select an area, any shape would work, including irregular shapes.

PhotoDeluxe, *PhotoHouse* and *PhotoImpact* have the facility whereby selections can be added to existing selections. This effect is simply random circles drawn with the circle selection tool. Providing the **Add** option is selected, as the circles overlap they will be added to the current selection.

When you've got the pattern you want, invert or reverse the selection and choose the effect you want to use. Because a colour/greyscale image couldn't be printed in a black and white book, this effect is negative.

PhotoDeluxe offers a very comprehensive assortment of adjustments from this dialog which can be accessed by clicking **Effects** on the menubar, going to **Extensis** on the drop down menu and choosing **Photo Frame** from the sub menu.

The list of possibilities is almost endless, but the main choice is between **Camera Edge**, **Water Colour Edge** and **Soft Circle**, which can be selected individually or used in any combination with each other.

The water colour frame works well with the water colour effect described on page 232 or with a normal picture as shown here.

Should you want to rotate the picture, you can do so, as well as vary the width, add blur, colour and opacity of the frame effect.

Vignette

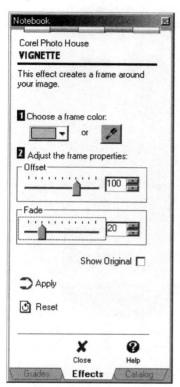

The Vignette feature in *PhotoHouse* can be accessed by clicking on **Effects** on the menubar, going to **Artistic Effects** on the drop down menu and choosing **Vignette...** from the sub menu.

Strictly speaking, a vignette is a head and shoulders picture, usually in an ellipse and frequently with an edge fade but there's no reason why you can't apply this effect to any picture.

The dialog gives the option of choosing a frame colour, which shouldn't be too bright unless you're using a black and white picture.

The **Offset** value can be entered as a number between 0 and 140, incremented by clicking on the up and down arrow alongside the number or dragging the slider along the scale. The **Offset** is the size of the ellipse. A value of zero will completely obliterate the picture whilst 140 will just shade the four corners.

The **Fade** value can be set in the same way and determines the amount of fade from zero (which has no fade whatsoever) to 100 which produces a large area of fade.

You must choose these values with care. You don't want to hide too much of the picture with either the offset or the fade. Begin with a light colour and set the Offset and the Fade to about halfway.

This vignette has an **Offset** value of 100 and a **Fade** value of only 10 which gives quite a narrow edge fade. This is because any more would begin to fade parts of the main subject.

A smaller offset would give flat sides to the ellipse which may be desirable, but if you are going to deliberately put flat spots on the edge ensure you do it enough so that it doesn't look like an accident.

Page Curl

This very popular edge effect is available in several programs although it wouldn't normally be printed, but rather used on screen – on a web page, for example. As the name implies, it is intended to give the impression that the page is curling up, but over-use can cause the viewer's lip to respond in a similar way.

In *PhotoHouse*, the dialog can be found by clicking on **Effects** on the menubar, going to **Cool & Fun Effects** on the drop down menu and choosing **Page Curl...** from the sub menu.

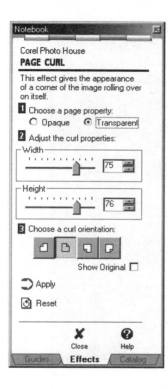

Once the Page Curl dialog is on-screen, there are three settings to be decided upon. The first is whether the curl is to be **Opaque** or **Transparent** and simply requires the appropriate button to be clicked. The second option requires a little more thought: you have to determine the distance along each side the effect is to begin. The example below used the settings shown in the dialog on the left. These settings were used to demonstrate the point, but for most purposes this would be too much.

Finally, the third option determines which corner the effect is to be applied to.

This simple dialog is effective and produces excellent results.

There are other programs that have this effect in their toolbox, but the most comprehensive version, called **Turnpage**, is found in *PhotoImpact*.

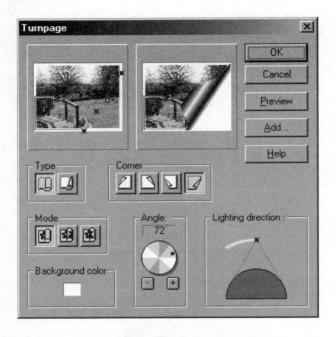

The thumbnail on the left of the dialog has a line with three nodes which can determine the angle and position of the curled corner. You can change the background colour and the amount the page is curled. This is given as **Angle** and is set by either dragging the wheel or clicking on the **+** and **−** buttons below the wheel.

As if that isn't enough, you can then adjust the **Lighting direction** which will determine where any highlight appears on the back of the scroll. The **Mode** button determines whether the scroll will be opaque, transparent so that you can see through the scroll onto the picture underneath, or transparent with the image printed on the back of the scroll (as in the example on the opposite page).

As with most effects, they are very clever if used in their original state or used in the way that they were originally intended. But you can get some better effects if you apply your imagination to them.

Selecting an area and applying a page curl to more than one corner gives the impression of a self-adhesive label which has been printed with a picture, but the picture has been printed onto the waste paper between the labels.

You'll need to read the section on Layers on page 177 and Opacity on page 191 to fully understand the way to build this picture. The picture on top was first put into *PhotoImpact* and given the page curl with a white background and as much shadow as possible. It was then saved and reopened in *PhotoDeluxe* where the background triangle, which includes the shadow cast by the page curl, was cut from the rest of the image, placed on a different layer and given a 40% opacity. Another picture was added and put on the backmost layer. The next layer has the semi-transparent triangle with the shadow and the first picture with the page curl is on top. The result is a page being turned to reveal another page underneath.

Page curl is a clever effect and initially has a high 'ooh-ah' factor. By that I mean when people first see it they go 'ooh-ah'. Shortly after they take little notice of it and shortly after that the effect is regarded as overly flashy.

Layers

What are layers?

The easiest way to describe layers is to think of a stack of transparent sheets. On each sheet is one 'thing' which is called an object. An object can be a whole drawing, part of a drawing or a piece of text. Not only can you move each layer relative to all the others, you can also scale the item on each layer independently of the others. But most important is that you can rearrange the order.

The tomato is on one layer whilst the lime is on another and the picture on the left clearly shows the lime in front of the tomato. By altering the order of the layers the tomato can clearly be seen to be in front of the lime. What is interesting is that all of both objects are present. The part of the tomato that was previously hidden by the lime can now be seen in the right picture.

In almost all cases, objects need to have a transparent background when working in layers. A full description of how to cut an object away from its background can be found in the section on page 131.

PhotoImpact and *PhotoHouse* handle layers in similar ways, although *PhotoHouse* refers to it as objects. *PhotoDeluxe* and *PerfectPhoto* both feature a layer toolbox which makes control of the layers much easier.

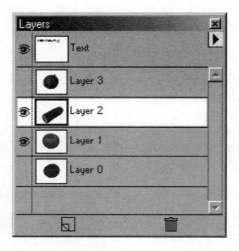

This toolbox is from *PhotoDeluxe*, but *PerfectPhoto*'s is similar. Each layer has a name (which defaults to Layer 0, Layer 1, Layer 2, etc.) and a thumbnail showing the contents of each layer. The layer shown in white is the one currently being worked on and the layers showing an eye in the left column are those which are currently visible in the picture window. Layers are made visible/invisible by clicking on the eye, and changing the layer to be worked on (the current layer) is achieved by clicking on the thumbnail.

Right clicking on the Layers dialog opens a menu with options including delete and create layer. Creating a new layer also happens automatically when a section from a drawing is copied and pasted into another.

Text is always placed on its own layer. You can place an almost unlimited amount of text on the text layer and each separate piece of text can be moved independently of the others.

The order of the objects in *PhotoHouse* can be changed by clicking **Objects** on the toolbar, and choosing one of four options.

With the Lime selected, **Back One Level** will place it between the Apple and the Tomato.

With the Tomato selected, **Send Object to Front** will place it in front of the Cucumber.

With the Apple selected, **Front One Level** will place it in front of the Lime, but behind the Cucumber.

With the Cucumber selected, **Send Object to Back** will place it behind the Tomato.

When moving objects in and out of the screen, you may need to adjust their horizontal position, but you will almost certainly need to adjust their vertical position as it may finish up looking as though some of the objects are floating in mid air.

Bringing the Tomato or the Apple to the front doesn't work without adjusting their vertical position. As it is, they look as though they're floating in mid air and the shadow below them is clearly wrong.

PhotoImpact uses four arrows on the toolbar to do exactly the same as the menus in *PhotoHouse*.

Remember, whichever application you're using, you must select the object you wish to move and then choose where you want to move it to.

Text

Most imaging software can handle text, but usually only for titles or annotation and is generally not designed to control huge blocks of text.

Click on the text tool which will usually open a small dialog into which you can enter the text and choose the font, fontsize and colour. When you've entered the text, it will be placed on the text layer when it can be resized, angled and positioned in the same way as any other object.

In the driving seat

Sometimes you have to cut a piece out of a picture and place it in a different layer.

The pictures of the model car and Biffer are going to be but as you will see, it's not simply a case of putting one picture on top of another. This effect was carried out in *PhotoDeluxe*, but it could equally have been done in *PhotoImpact*, *PerfectPhoto*, *PhotoHouse* or any image editing application which supports layers and objects. The background was removed from around Biffer and, because a different background was going to be added later, the existing background was removed from around the car.

Select the part of the first picture (Biffer) and paste it into the other picture (the car). (Read the section on page 155 for an explanation of copying and pasting.)

Pasting Biffer into the picture of the car creates a new layer.

The two pictures are different sizes: the dog is clearly far too big for the car and so the next task is to change the size of one so they are in scale with each other. It is almost always preferable to reduce the size of one rather than increase the size of the other, as increasing the size can lead to an effect known as pixelation. Hold down the CTRL key when you drag a corner node to ensure the aspect ratio remains the same. (Refer to the Glossary on page 277 for explanations of aspect ratio and pixelation.)

There are no tools to help to get two images to the same scale - you just have to use your judgement to get it right.

When Biffer is in the correct position, he should obscure the seats and much of the inside of the car. Yet as it is, he will be partly obscuring the door nearest to the viewer indicating that he is outside the car.

To make it look like Biffer is inside the car, the door will need to be cut out, placed on in front of Biffer.

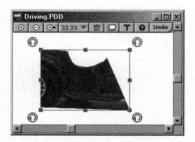

Use a freehand cutting tool and mark around a suitable area. Cut it and paste it back and it will create a new layer containing just the section removed from the car.

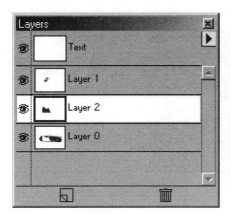

Apart from the text layer, you'll have three layers: a dog (Layer1), a door (Layer2) and a car with a big hole in the side (Layer0). They need to be shuffled so that the car is at the bottom, Biffer in the middle and the door on top.

Select Layer 0 (the car), open the layer menu and send it to the back. Then, select Layer 1 (the door) and bring it to the front.

When you display all of the layers you should see the car with Biffer sitting inside.

In the driving seat...

The full explanation of how this picture came about is in the section on backgrounds on page 185. This is another example of objects being arranged in layers. Originally there were two pictures: Simon standing by a parking space and a toy car.

The two photographs were taken with this effect specifically in mind and so the camera angles for the two pictures were, as near as possible, the same. Even so, the car had to be rotated slightly to make it look as though it really had been parked on the drive.

Sometimes, the size of the piece which has to be placed on another layer is so small, you may be forgiven for thinking that the time taken to complete the task is not worth the small amount of detail that would be lost. Not so. In the picture on the right showing me holding an illuminated

light bulb that is apparently not connected to any power supply, the only section that needed to be moved from the main picture was the first section of the index finger. This had to be placed in front of the bulb. Had the finger not been cut out and replaced, the trick would have been lost.

Backgrounds

Changing the backdrop

One of the problems many amateur photographers have is what is behind the subject. All too often we spend time lining up the subject, making sure it's in focus, and when the picture has been printed you notice something in the background you don't like. If the photograph was taken with a film camera, there's not very much you can do about it. If it's been taken with a digital camera, (or you've got a photograph which has been scanned to produce a digital image) then you can make major alterations to the background, including completely replacing it.

How is it done?

Regardless of whether you wish to alter, replace or remove the background, you will need to separate the foreground from the background. Depending on what the background is like, will depend whether you use a magic wand tool or a freehand cutting tool. See the section on cutting tools on page 131.

This model Jaguar was photographed on a grey table top. It was opened in PerfectPhoto and the Magic Wand tool was used to remove most of the background. The cutting tool was used to clean up the odd pixels left behind.

The chequered area in *PerfectPhoto* indicates that the background colour is transparent: a vital feature if you're going to place the picture over another without obliterating the picture at the back. (See the section on page 177 for an explanation of layers.)

This job usually has to be done using one image editing tool only as it's frequently difficult to transfer pictures with special features like transparent backgrounds between applications whilst maintaining the transparent effect. You must save your work in a format which supports layers and transparent areas and the file formats which support these are not usually transferable between different applications. (See page 37 for an explanation of different filetypes.)

New background

When you have removed the background, you will need to open a new document containing the background you wish to use. You can either shoot the new background yourself or use one of thousands available on the Internet.

Many of the image editing applications are supplied with a library of pictures, including dozens of backgrounds. *PerfectPhoto* is typical. When the application is installed you have the option of also installing the image library which contains over 100 high quality pictures which can be used for backgrounds.

You will almost certainly need to scale the foreground image to match the background. Get it scaled approximately before putting it onto the background.

When you've got the scale about right, the foreground can be copied and pasted onto the background. (See page 155 for an explanation of copying and pasting.)

Once there, it can been slid into position and the size adjusted.

When choosing a background, or shooting one yourself, it's important to try to get the camera angle as close as possible to the angle the foreground was shot at.

The picture on the left looks wrong and the reason is that the foreground and the background were shot with different camera angles. The background (which was supplied with *PerfectPhoto*) was probably shot with the camera almost horizontal, whereas Biffer was photographed with the camera pointing down at about 20° - 30°. What really exaggerates this is the dog basket. If this picture were shot as a single photograph, you wouldn't be able to see so much of the inside of Biffer's basket.

The give-away is the basket and if this is removed it's more convincing, but it's still not quite right.

When undertaking projects like this, a good deal of work is involved. Although you may only need to remove part of, say, a person from a picture, removing all of the person might mean you can use that cut-out elsewhere. In short, a little more work now might mean a substantial saving later.

Distracting backgrounds

You can create some unusual and interesting effects by removing the subject in the foreground, applying an effect to the background and then replacing the subject.

These orchids were removed from the picture and the background was then blurred before they were replaced. This treatment makes the subject stand out from the picture by making the background less distracting.

The opposite also applies. You can take a mundane background and make it more interesting by applying some of the effects described in the section on blurring and softening on page 109 or pixelating on page 121. There is also the section on hand colouring on page 85 which might be useful when disguising backgrounds.

Opacity

See through

When an object is covered or partly covered by another, it's hidden because it's opaque – you can't see through it. But you can make objects transparent or partly transparent enabling you to see through them. (You'll need to read the section on layers on page 177 before attempting anything in this section.)

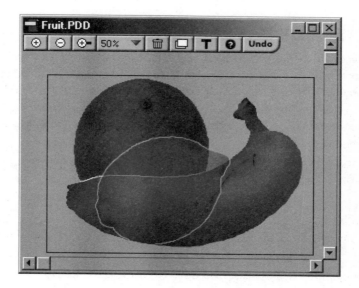

To make it easier to see, the lemon and the banana have been outlined in white. The lemon has been made semi-transparent. Although it's in front of both the banana and the orange, you can see all of the banana and as much of the orange as isn't covered by the banana, which is still opaque.

Each layer in PerfectPhoto has the facility to determine the degree of transparency. The default value is 0 which is solid and totally opaque, whilst 100 is totally invisible. This dialog appears when you double click on the layer palette, with the mouse pointer over the layer which you want to adjust. The pointer can be dragged over the scale or a number entered in the box to the right.

A spirit from the past?

There are lots of photographs which claim to show the existence of ghosts. Most are undoubtedly fake. As to the rest, I leave an open mind. Creating such pictures is a great deal easier with digital processing software: especially if you have a transparency feature like *PhotoHouse*, *PhotoImpact* or you can control opacity as you can in *PhotoDeluxe* or *PerfectPhoto*.

If you want to create this effect, it can be as simple as placing a semi-transparent image on top of another image so that you can see through the top image.

First, use a selection tool to select the figure and remove it from its background, which can then be discarded. (For more information about selecting, read the section on page 131.)

Find a suitable background and place it on one layer, and the figure on another. (Information about layers in on page 177.)

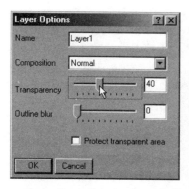

Give the figure a transparency of about 40% (or an opacity of 60%, depending which program you're using) and ensure the figure is in front of the background. To make it a little more realistic, in the example on the previous page part of the banister was cut out and placed in front of the figure.

Although adding a semi-transparent figure over a different background works quite well, a better result can be obtained by adding edge fading to the image which will give the effect of it glowing.

Magnifying glass

I saw this magnifying glass and thought I'd like to photograph it, although at that stage I hadn't any idea what I was going to use it for. It was photographed in a conservatory and caught several reflections from above. Note the reflection from the window near to the handle and the highlight at the top of the lens.

The background was separated from the magnifying glass using a freehand selection tool and the lens was then removed from the frame in the same way, and placed on another layer.

The lens then had a 30% opacity applied to it. In *PhotoDeluxe* this dialog can be found by double clicking on the layer dialog.

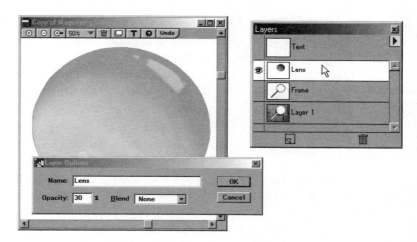

The trouble with this picture as it stands is that because there isn't anything under the lens, you can't see whether it's transparent of not.

The scanned postage stamp was placed behind both the lens and the frame of the magnifying glass. As with most work of this type, the stamp needed to be removed from its background. Using a freehand selection tool and tracing around the object would

have been difficult and time consuming. To ensure an automatic selection tool (like a *PerfectPhoto*'s Magic Wand) would work quickly and accurately, the stamp was scanned against a black background. The high contrast between the black of the background and the white of the stamp ensured a very accurate outline.

The stamp (without its background) was then rotated behind the glass to give the most interesting effect. The lens is slightly tinted which makes the part of the stamp that's behind the lens a slightly different colour to the part of the stamp that's outside the lens.

To improve the effect the part of the stamp under the lens can be enlarged to attempt to show a degree of magnification. The part of the stamp under the lens was separated from the rest of the stamp. When doing this, you don't need to be very accurate when tracing around with a freehand cutting tool like *PhotoDeluxe*'s Polygon Selection tool as the join between the two parts of the stamp will be behind the frame of the magnifying glass.

Note the reflections on the glass are still present and the colour of the stamp underneath the reflections is slightly different.

The part of the stamp under the lens can then be enlarged. Of course, you wouldn't really see this degree of magnification with the stamp being so close to the lens. It's called artistic licence!

Modelling glasses

When Prime Minister Blair arrived at a conference wearing a pair of glasses for the first time, one paper suggested that his glasses were rather bland and that he could have chosen other, more adventurous designs. To illustrate the point, the newspaper showed him wearing glasses more commonly associated with personalities like Elton John and Dame Edna Everage.

The technique used for putting different glasses on a face is not dissimilar to that used for the magnifying glass.

Begin by getting a suitable full face picture. Before fitting the glasses, I cut Steve from the background, blurred the background slightly and put him back.

Each of the glasses were then cut away from their backgrounds, and the backgrounds discarded. For more information about removing sections of a picture, read the section on selecting on page 131.

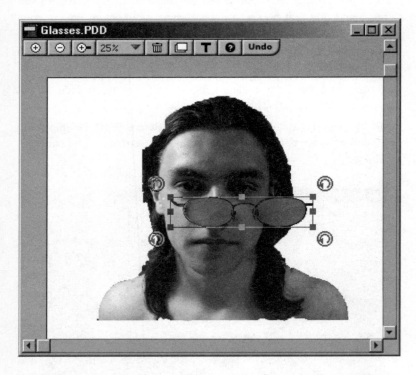

Inevitably, the picture of the glasses will be too big for the face or vice versa. The general rule is to reduce the larger one to fit, where possible. If the glasses are too big, reduce them to fit the face rather than scaling the face up to fit the glasses. (Bit map images like these do not scale well, especially if you try to enlarge them.)

When the glasses fit the face, and only when they do, should you attempt to remove the lenses. There are several tools that could be used for this job, but because of the high contrast between the lens and frame, a tool like *PerfectPhoto*'s Magic Wand should work well.

If you have the facility to add selections together or add to an existing selection then use this feature to keep the two lenses together. When they have been marked, cut them and paste them back. (Read about cutting and pasting on page 155.) This will have separated the lenses from the frames and placed them on different layers. When you paste them you may have to move them slightly to get them lined up to the frames.

Like the magnifying glass, you'll need to put a degree of transparency to the lenses so that you will be able to see the eyes through them.

Even though Steven has never worn these glasses (he couldn't if he wanted to – they're his brother's and far too small for him) you can get a good idea what he looks like with them.

One high street optician had a similar idea on their website where you could upload a photograph of yourself and 'try on' a variety of their spectacles from the comfort of your own home.

Varying the degree of opacity can change the effect, but notice how the highlight still remains on the lens even though you can now see through them.

Distortions

Special effects

Not long ago, techniques such as this were beyond the power of most people's computers, unless you were prepared to wait for a considerable period of time whilst the calculations were carried out. All of the featured programs offer some element of picture distortion either to correct a problem with the picture or to produce a specific effect.

Perspective

If you take a close-up picture of a large object you'll capture the perspective effect of perfectly vertical walls appearing to slope down towards the ground. In the example of the Houses of Parliament, taken from the London Eye, all vertical lines appear to converge at what is usually referred to as the vanishing point.

To remove this effect and put the vertical lines back to vertical requires a degree of picture distortion. You can't simply rotate the picture so that Big Ben is vertical, because to other walls will be even further out.

PerfectPicture has the perfect solution for this. In the Transformation tools is a tool called Perspective. To get to this dialog, choose **Layer** from the drop down menu and then select **Transform...** .

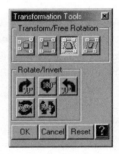

When Perspective is selected, a box is drawn around the picture with a node at each corner. Each node works with the opposite one so that if you drag the top left node towards the right, the top right node will move towards the left by the same amount.

Move the nodes in small steps. You probably won't be able to get all vertical lines truly vertical, indeed this may not be desirable as it could lead to the image looking false. You can easily check for verticalness (if there is such a term) by comparing a long vertical line with the side of the window.

When you've got the vertical lines as vertical as possible, you'll need to crop the image to make the picture rectangular again.

This effect has been used by advertisers, almost since the dawn of advertising. Rather than trying to correct the perspective, you can use the same tool to exaggerate it.

Pinch and Punch

These effects are available in most programs, including those featured in this book, but *PhotoHouse* seems to offer the most control. The idea is that if you pinch a piece of the picture and pull it out, you'll distort the area around where you've pinched. Punch is the opposite because the distortion looks as though it's going in to the picture, rather than coming out.

To access this feature in *PhotoHouse*, click on **Effects** on the menubar, go to **Distortion Effects** on the drop down menu and select **Pinch/Punch...** from the sub menu.

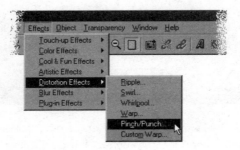

The control will appear on the left side of the window. Using the mouse, drag the slider to the left or right to control the amount of pinch or punch.

Swirl and Ripple

These effects are similar to each other, both invariably leave the image totally unrecognisable. As with Pinch and Punch, *PhotoHouse* provides the greatest degree of control. You can very the number of ripples or swirls and their depth.

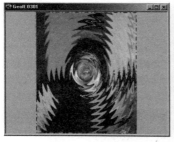 

In most programs, including *PhotoHouse*, that have this feature, you'll find it in the same place as Pinch and Punch.

The slider is dragged using the mouse. Move the mouse pointer onto the slider, press and hold the left mouse button and drag the slider from side to side. When you release the mouse button the calculation, based on the current value is performed on the picture.

When you've got the picture as you want it, click on **Apply**. At any time you can revert to the original image by clicking on the **Show Original** tickbox.

You can also access this dialog by clicking on the **Guides** tab at the foot of the panel, choosing **Prepare Image**, selecting background followed by **Next**, **Whole Image** followed by **Next**, **Distortion** and then the distorting feature you require.

Warp

Providing lots of control is not always the best solution. *PhotoHouse* offers very little control over its warp feature. You can choose to 'wrap' the picture around either a horizontal or vertical cylinder, or as is shown here, a sphere. In both cases the picture can be concave (inside) or convex (outside).

Like Swirl and Ripple, this feature is also found in the distortion menu. Note that the term 'sphere' is something of a misnomer. The software will place the largest possible ellipse into the picture. If the picture happens to be square, you'll get a sphere. If not, it'll be a flattened sphere.

By contrast, *PhotoImpact* provides a grid onto which you can adjust nodes to achieve the desired effect.

This feature requires a considerable amount of patience to get a satisfactory result. The feature is found by clicking on **Effect** on the menubar and choosing **Warping...** from the drop down menu. This opens a dialog showing the current image with a grid covering it. Each intersection on the grid is a node which can be dragged anywhere within the area. The thumbnail at the bottom shows what the finished picture will look like.

Mirage

This effect is available in many imaging applications, but this particular effect was created in *PerfectPhoto*.

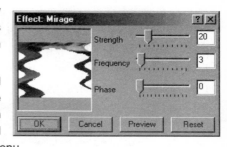

The mirage effect can be found by going to **Effects** on the menubar, going to **Effects** on the drop down menu and selecting **Mirage...** on the sub menu.

This interesting effect was created by removing Biffer from the picture, applying the Mirage effect to the background and then putting the picture back together.

To complete a picture like this, you'll need to read the section on selecting on page 131 and background editing on page 185.

Crystal ball

The Dutch artist M.C.Escher studied this effect in depth and produced some supurb drawings, including one of himself holding a glass sphere carrying his own distorted reflection.

For this effect I used *PhotoImpact* and *PerfectPhoto*.

If you want to create this effect with a perfect sphere, you'll need to begin with a square picture. If the picture is rectangular, you'll get an ellipse rather than a circle.

Open the picture you want to work with into *PhotoImpact*. Choose the Sphere tool by clicking **Effect** on the menubar, going to **3D** and choosing **Sphere...** from the sub menu.

A window will pop up showing three variations. You may select different lighting effects by clicking on the **Options** button and when you've got the preview as you want it, press **OK**.

PhotoImpact creates the sphere in the centre of the picture and leaves the four corners in place. If you want to remove the corners to leave just the sphere, you need an application which will provide an elliptical or circular cutting tool.

PerfectPhoto has an elliptical selection tool, as does *PhotoImpact* and *PhotoDeluxe*) which can outline a perfect circle. From the **Tools** dialog, choose the Ellipse tool.

When *PhotoImpact* created the sphere effect, it put the largest possible circle into the photograph. So, to select all of the sphere you'll need to start in the very top left corner and drag to the far bottom right hand corner.

From this point you can go two ways. The neatest way is to invert the selection by clicking on the toolbox icon.

This makes everything that was selected, unselected and everything that was previously unselected the current selection. Press **Delete** to remove the current selection and you're left with the sphere.

The alternative method, once you've selected the circle, is to copy the selected image (eg the sphere), create a new document which is at least as large as the square photograph you started with, and paste the sphere onto a white background. Read the section on page 155 to find out more about cutting and pasting.

Rotate, Flip & Mirror

Rotate

Sometimes, because the subject is taller than it is wide, it makes sense to hold the camera at 90° to take the picture. To view the picture on screen, you might prefer to rotate it to its correct orientation rather than turn your head 90° or lay the monitor on its side.

A photo taken with the camera on its side like this makes for a better composition, but you'll need to rotate it to its correct orientation when you get it on screen.

Microsoft's *PhotoEditor* provides this facility via a dialog with a rather clever graphic that shows you exactly what will happen to your image.

Choose **Image** on the menubar and then click on **Rotate...** on the drop down menu.

The basic rotations are 90° left (or anticlockwise), 90° right (or clockwise) and transpose (rotate by 180°). Click on the button on the left, check with the graphic that the image is going to rotate the way you want it to, and click on **OK**.

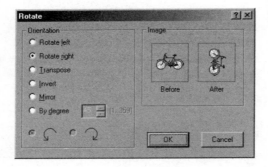

PhotoHouse by contrast offers the choice of either selecting rotation from a menu or from Guided Activities.

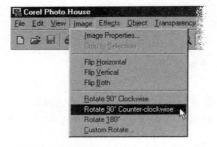

From the menubar, choose **Image** and then either **90° Clockwise, 90° Counter clockwise** (or anticlockwise) or **Rotate 180°** which turns the image upside down.

If you get the rotation wrong, you can either press **CTRL Z** to undo the last alteration, or choose another orientation. The most likely mistake you'll make here is to rotate by 90° in the wrong direction. The easiest way to correct the mistake and get the picture into the correct orientation is to choose **Rotate 180°**.

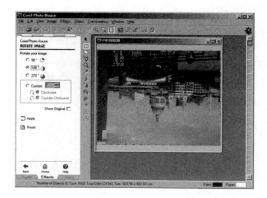

PhotoHouse also offers rotation via the **Guided Activities**. Choose **Prepare Image** and then **Transform Image**. Finally, click on **Apply** to rotate the image by the selected amount.

If you're using *PerfectPhoto*, choose **Image** from the menubar and then **Rotation...** followed by either **90 degrees right**, **90 degrees left** or **180 degrees**.

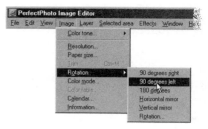

Kodak's *Imaging* offers just two rotations which are via icons on the toolbar. The choice is either rotate left by 90° or rotate right 90°.

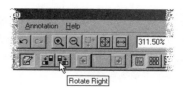

Arbitrary rotation

I've yet to find a program that doesn't offer the option of rotating a photo through 90° or a multiple of 90°. The ability to turn a picture through an arbitrary amount is less common. This is a particularly handy feature, especially if, like me, you don't always hold the camera exactly horizontally.

No, not the result of a liquid lunch, nor was it a very windy day. It's easy to get a picture slightly off true horizontal especially when you haven't got a reference point.

PhotoHouse offers the user the chance to rotate an image in units of 1° either clockwise or anticlockwise, as does *PhotoEditor*, *PerfectPhoto* and *PhotoImpact*.

Arbitrary rotation in *PhotoHouse* can be accessed from the menubar by selecting **Image** and choosing **Custom Rotate...** .

This will open the **Guide Activities** and you can enter a number of whole degrees (no decimal places are allowed). Click the button to choose the direction of rotation and click **Apply**.

PhotoImpact refers to this facility as the transform tool and it can be found by going to **Edit** on the menubar, choosing **Rotate and Flip** on the drop down menu and then clicking on **Transform Tool** at the bottom of the sub menu.

An extra tool appears on the toolbar where you enter a number of whole degrees in the panel and then click on the clockwise or anticlockwise icon to rotate the picture.

Drag rotate

Entering a number is not always the easiest way to straighten up an image. It can be a matter of trial and error to get it right. If you're not interested in how many degrees the image is to be rotated, then use *PhotoDeluxe*.

From the menubar in *PhotoDeluxe*, choose **Orientation** and from the drop down menu choose **Free Rotate** and handles will appear at the four corners of the picture. Click on any of the handles and drag the picture around until you've got it as you want it.

This feature is particularly useful with scanned images where they frequently need a small amount of rotation to get them exactly true.

Flip and mirror

Most picture editors, including the six featured in this book, offer the user the facility to flip and mirror images. Flip is sometimes referred to top to bottom transposition or vertical transposition. This is not the same as rotating by 180° as the resulting image will be rather like an upside-down mirror image. Mirror is rather like turning the page of a book. It's also often referred to as horizontal transposition.

The photo of this watch demonstrates the point. Consider the position of the crown wheel (the winder), the date and the actual time shown on the watch.

The same picture has been transformed in three different ways. The picture on the left has been flipped vertically. The winder is still on the right but if you look at the date, you'll see that apart from being upside down, the number '2' is mirrored. The middle picture has been mirrored or horizontally flipped. Note the top of the watch is still at the top, but the winder has moved to the left. This is the view you would see if you looked at the watch in a mirror. (To prove this point, look at this picture in a mirror and it will appear the correct way round.) By contrast, the picture on the right has been rotated by 180°.

The flip and mirror functions are usually found in the same place as rotate. In *PhotoEditor*, for example, Invert and Mirror can be found on the **Rotate** dialog whereas the other applications provide them as options on the **Edit** drop down menu.

Symmetrical face?

You can make some interesting effects with these functions. One might think that a face is symmetrical, but here's an interesting test you can perform to prove that that is almost certainly not the case. Take a photograph of someone you think has a symmetrical face.

Take the photograph full on, in other words, so that the camera is not angled towards one side of the face.

Select the right hand side of the face, make a copy (press **CTRL C**), mirror it and re-position it carefully over the left side of the face so that you have two right hand sides. Assume the centre of the nose as the line on which to select half of the image.

When you've got the original picture, a picture containing two left halves and another containing two right halves you'll see that even the most symmetrical face has two quite different sides.

T Shirt

A popular fashion is T Shirts with pictures on them. Many shops provide the service and it's very popular at seaside resorts where you can have a holiday snap put onto your T Shirt. If you've got a camera or scanner and a good printer, you've got almost everything you need to do the job yourself.

The key to this project is a pack of iron-on transfer sheets which several companies produce including Epson and Hewlett Packard.

When you've got your picture you should first print it on plain paper to check that it fits - mistakes on the iron-on film are expensive.

When you're ready to print your picture onto the film, you must first mirror it. It is in this form that it will be printed onto the film and when it has been ironed on to the garment, it will be the correct way round.

When printing, use the best quality setting on your printer. Many printers have a setting for film, and some even have a special setting for iron-on film. Check this by clicking on **Printer Properties** from the printer dialog which can be accessed by pressing **CTRL P**.

When ironing the picture onto the garment, use a low setting on the iron. Go over the transfer several times and you should be able to see when the transfer has gone onto the garment as the picture will go slightly lighter.

Kaleidoscope

There are several ways to create a kaleidoscope pattern, but I found the most straightforward way is using *PhotoImpact*. Even within *PhotoImpact*, there is more than one way. This is my preferred method, you might find another way that suits you better.

This composition of lentils and sesame seeds doesn't look very promising but it can be turned into a very interesting pattern quite easily.

The first step is to crop the image so that the pattern reaches the left vertical and the bottom edges of the picture. It doesn't matter if you lose part of the pattern – it just adds to the final effect.

Next, create a blank page which is approximately the same proportions as the cropped picture. In most cases, to create a new document, click on **New** on the menubar and enter the dimensions of the new blank page into the dialog.

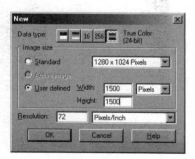

Drag and drop the cropped picture into your new file and click on it to select it. Now, alter the dimensions of the selected image so that it occupies approximately ¼ of the new picture. To alter the dimensions, click on **Format** on the menubar and choose **Dimensions...** . A dialog will open into which you can enter a percentage by which to reduce or increase the picture. Before you click **OK**, ensure you have clicked the **Keep Aspect Ratio** tickbox. This will ensure that the proportions of the picture remain the same.

Drag the image to the top right of the new picture.

Make a copy of the selected image (**CTRL C**) and then paste it into the same area (**CTRL V**). The copied image will now be the selected area and this should be flipped horizontally and then dragged into position alongside the top right section. You may need to magnify the view so that you can locate it exactly without overlapping and without a white space between them.

Now copy each of the two existing pieces and flip them vertically. When these are in position, you should have a kaleidoscope pattern.

Remarkably, a non-computerised version of this process has been in use for several centuries. Cabinet makers used this concept to match wood veneers which were used on cabinets. Book-match veneering involved selecting veneers, which were cut from the same log, and opening them up like a book so that the left side mirrors the right side.

To take the concept yet further, *PerfectPhoto* actually has a facility called Kaleidoscope which does much of this for you. You can select the number of reflections, which the program will divide into 360° and so complete a circle of pieces of the original image.

Begin by choosing your picture and placing it into a blank document which is considerably larger than the image. The Kaleidoscope effect can be found by choosing **Effects** on the menubar, going to **Effects** on the drop down menu and choosing **Kaleidoscope...** from the sub menu.

This opens a dialog into which you must enter the number of **Reflections**. In the area on the right you can drag the circle to choose the centre of the pattern and how much of the picture will be used in the pattern. The thumbnail on the left shows what the picture will look like. When you've got it as you want it, click on **OK**.

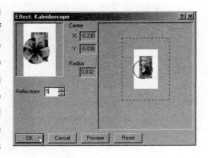

To finish off the picture, choose the circle selection tool and mark a circle around the picture. The selection can then be copied (**CTRL C**) and pasted into another picture (**CTRL V**).

Filters

Through the lens

If you go to a photography shop, amongst all the different gadgets you can buy for your camera (film camera or digital camera) are filters. These are fitted in front of the lens to create a particular effect. Many of these effects, and several others, can be simulated in a digital imaging application.

Coloured filters

If you place a coloured filter in front of the lens, the picture will acquire that colour. A blue lens, for example, will make many of the colours in the photo a shade of blue.

In certain situations a filter can lift the picture. The photograph of the London Eye, for example, was taken on a particularly drab day, but giving it a blue filter makes it look much less depressing.

This effect can be found in Microsoft's *PhotoEditor* by choosing **Image** on the menubar and selecting **Balance** from the drop down menu which will open a dialog.

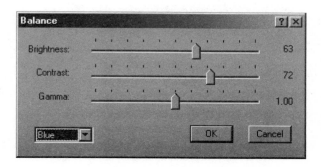

At the bottom left is a drop down menu which gives the user the opportunity to make adjustments to all colours, or to select individual colours.

This particularly drab photo is not made any more cheerful in black and white. A blue filter makes the sky bluer – even the dark thundercloud in the top right looks more inviting.

PhotoDeluxe has a similar feature which can be used simulate different coloured filters placed in front of the lens.

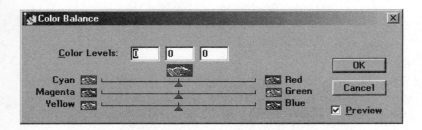

The three sliders can adjust overall colour of a photograph to produce widely different effects.

For more about colour, read the section on page 67.

Lens refraction

PhotoShop has this subtle trick in its armoury which resembles the refraction of light through a camera lens and produces a spot of light and a rainbow effect just outside the highlight.

This effect can be found by choosing **Effects** on the menubar, going to **Cool & Fun Effects** on the drop down menu and clicking on **Lens Refraction** on the sub menu. The dialog gives the user the choice of where to place the highlight, the colour of the refraction and the size of the lens that created the refraction.

When applying this effect, you should place the centre of the refraction on something that would normally reflect light. In the example, the light is on the silver corner of the phone's screen and one could imagine the effect occurring naturally.

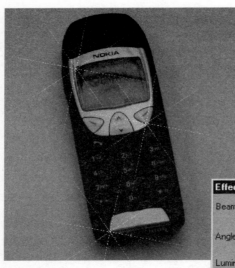

A similar effect is found in *PerfectPhoto*. The **Cross** effect places a cross or star of light on the picture. This effect attempts to duplicate the star filter which is a popular accessory with serious photographers. Although you can place

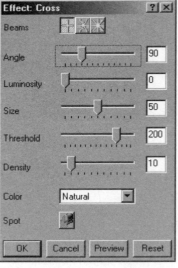

as many stars as you wish, in practice two or three is usually ample. Any more and the picture just looks a mess.

There are seven options in the dialog which can be found by choosing **Effects** on the menubar, going to **Photo** on the drop down menu and clicking on **Cross** from the sub menu.

This effect really must be placed at an intersection or corner of a high-gloss item for it to be convincing. In the illustration, the stars are placed at the top inside edge of the screen surround, the corner of a key and the corner of the silver trim at the bottom of the phone. If the photograph had been taken with a star filter over the lens these are the most likely places the stars would be occur.

This trick can also be used to good effect on a smiling face with a star placed on a tooth. Next time you see a toothpaste advertisement, look to see how many times you see this effect.

Multi-image

PerfectPhoto's multi-image is a superb effect which can produce dramatic results.

When the dialog is opened, there are basically four settings that need to be decided.

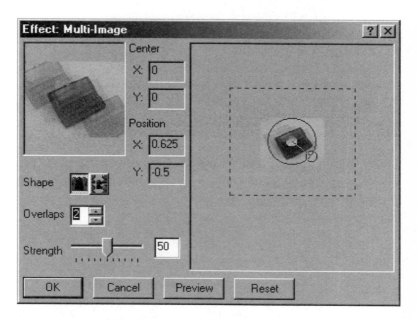

The number placed in the **Overlaps** box determines how many images will appear with the main image. The strength of the image determines how bold the additional images will be. The circles in the graphic on the right of the dialog determine the amount of the image that is to be copied and the direction of the copies. The Shape refers to the pattern of the multiple images and can be either be in a straight line or in a square as shown in the example on the next page.

This effect works best with a bold image on a plain background, but you can get some interesting effects by selecting an area before making a multi-image.

After marking around the foreground, the selection was subjected to the multi-image effect which then only works within the selected area.

If you're going to try this, wear white so the additional images can be clearly seen.

Artistic Effects

Paint effects

This is a simple idea and one that is used in most digital imaging
applications with varying degrees of success. These effects are
intended to make your digital photograph look like it has been hand
painted or coloured by hand.

Oil

PerfectPhoto's oil effect is about the best of the five applications mainly
used in this book. With the right subject, it can look quite convincing.
The dialog is found by clicking on **Effects** on the menubar, going to
Effects on the drop down menu and choosing **Oil painting...** from the
sub menu.

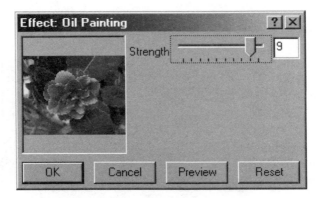

The dialog provides the user with just one function: how strong to make
the effect. The trick is, if you are going to use it, be bold and set it high.

Water

PhotoImpact's water colour is one of the best effects of this type, but will take a lot of experimenting to get really good results.

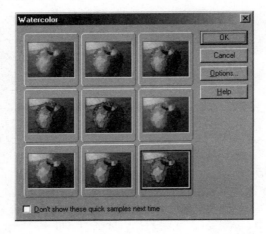

When you get the picture as you want it, it can be further enhanced by adding a water colour frame which can be found in *PhotoDeluxe*.

Chalk and Charcoal

This *PhotoDeluxe* effect tries to simulate a drawing done with chalk. There is no opportunity for adjusting the effect: once you've selected it, the process begins. You can, however, choose the foreground colour (chalk) and the background colour

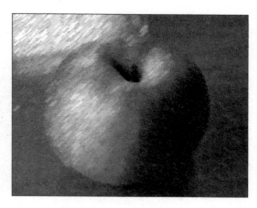

(charcoal). If you find the result doesn't look quite as you expected, try choosing photo negative which may improve the appearance.

Pencil

One of the easiest effects to work with is the coloured pencil in *PhotoDeluxe*. Unlike the previous effect, choosing **Coloured Pencil...** from the **Artistic** menu opens a dialog which has three sliders to adjust pencil width, stroke pressure and paper brightness.

But before getting to the dialog, choose the pencil colours from the menu which can have a dramatic effect on the final result.

This is another effect that requires lots of experimentation to get right. Not only will you need to change the values in the dialog, but you'll also need to choose your picture carefully. The flower seems to have worked well but I failed to get any reasonable results with the apple.

Wet paint

Of all the effects in all of the applications, my favourite is the dripping wet paint found in *PhotoHouse*, although I'm not sure where it might be used.

You can find this effect by choosing **Effect** on the menubar, going to **Cool & Fun Effect** on the drop down menu and choosing **Wet Paint...** from the sub menu to open the dialog. Alternatively, you can get to the same dialog by following through the **Guided Activities** panel on the left.

Chrome

Another effect worth looking out for is Chrome which can be found in *PhotoDeluxe*. With the right picture, this can produce an amazing black chrome look.

Sketch

This is easily the best effect of this type and is found in *PhotoHouse* by going to **Effects** on the menubar, going to **Artistic Effects** on the drop down menu and clicking on **Sketch...** on the sub menu.

A dialog opens where you can choose either soft or solid line and a slider which determines the density of the image. *PhotoHouse*'s sketch effect gives good results on just about any picture, but technical items look especially good.

Even though the pictures shown here have been reduced, you can still see a lot of detail on the watch (above) and although the legends on the phone keys (right) are not really legible, you can see some of the numbers.

These pictures usually look best if they are converted into black and white after being sketched.

Modern art

There are many clever effects that you can incorporate into your pictures. These include blurring the background, soft focus and the use of filters to 'wash' the picture in a particular colour. Many of these effects can be reproduced with digital image editing software, but these applications can also be used to create some amazing effects that can't be done using conventional photographic techniques. But as clever as these effects are, the real trick is knowing when to use them.

Electrify

This effect which is found in *PhotoHouse*, I presume, is intended to look like the subject has been chained to the National Grid overnight.

It basically changes whites into electric shades of blue and green. It's a little like a photographic negative in parts, but darker shades are unaffected which is why the shirt (which was white) has changed, as have the highlights on the arm and hand. The rest of the photo is unchanged.

Psychedelic

A variation on this theme is the Psychedelic effect also found in *PhotoHouse*.

Rather than changing some colours like the electrify effect, psychedelic changes all of them. You can increase the intensity of the effect which gives darker colours. This is a very dramatic effect and needs to be seen in colour to fully appreciate it.

Sponge

A sponge is an increasingly popular tool for decorating and now you can bring this effect to your digital pictures if you have *PhotoDeluxe*.

When this option is chosen, a dialog opens in which you can choose the size of the sponge and the definition of the sponge.

Notepaper

PhotoDeluxe's notepaper effect produces an image rather like a watermark. This is not to be confused with the black and white only effect of threshold (see page 79) as this also gives a textured effect rather like pebbledash wallpaper.

Emboss

This effect seems almost obligatory in photo editing software. Most applications offer some control over the process, like *PerfectPhoto* which gives the user the choice of light direction and depth.

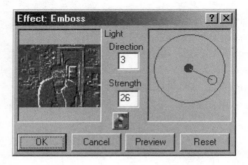

Although this process works quite well with photographs, it is much better with text effects. With the right depth of relief and the correct colour this effect can easily be made to look like the picture has been cast in pewter.

Text Effects

Applying text

Although photo editing applications are primarily designed to handle pictures, many can also display a limited amount of text. In general, text is restricted to titles and labels which can be applied in a variety of interesting ways.

Kodak's *Imaging* is one of the best applications for applying text to a picture. At the bottom of the *Imaging* window is a toolbar with 10 buttons to access various annotation features.

If the lower toolbar is not present, click on **View** on the menubar at the top of the window, go to **Toolbars...** on the drop down menu and ensure **Annotation** is ticked on the dialog.

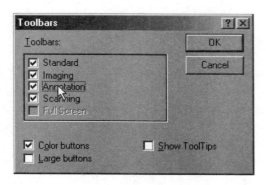

Right hand clicking on any of the icons on the annotation toolbar (except the arrow on the extreme left) will open a menu containing just one item: **Properties**. Clicking on this will open a dialog which will allow you to set the default values for each of the buttons. The text button, for example, opens a dialog from which you can choose the standard font, font size and colour.

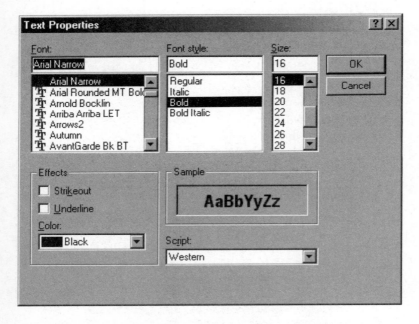

It is important to begin setting the default values as this will ensure a degree of consistency between pictures you are labelling.

Applying text directly onto a photograph is not always the best way as it's frequently is difficult to read. *Imaging* allows you to place the text in a coloured rectangle. You can apply either a solid rectangle or an outline rectangle, and then type onto the box, but the quickest and simplest way is to **Add a note**.

Click on the ▢ icon and then position the cursor on the drawing. When you type, an outlined box will be drawn in the pre-determined colour. As you continue to type, the box will automatically expand to accommodate the text.

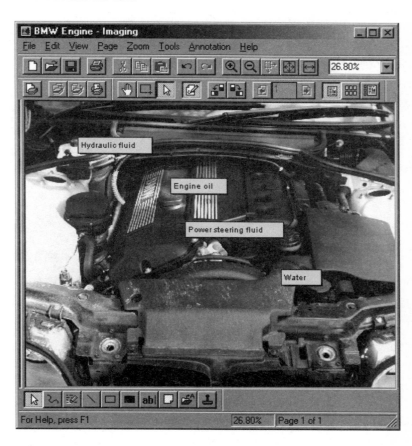

Once you've entered a label, click on the arrow icon, select a label by clicking on it and dragging it into the exact position you want.

If you want a label with a background, but you don't want the background rectangle to obliterate too much of the picture, you can choose a highlighter which is basically a semi-transparent rectangle which can also be used for highlighting a particular feature of your picture. The highlight box can just be seen in this black and white picture which shows another text handling feature of *Imaging*: text from a file.

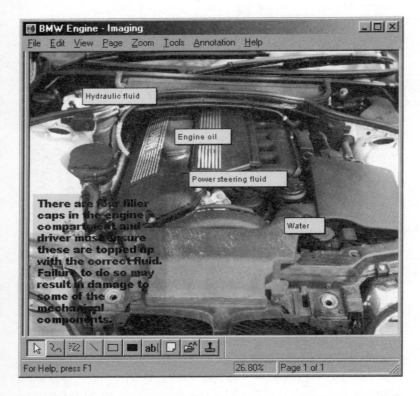

If you want to include a larger amount of text (ie more than one or two words) you can still type them directly onto your picture, but the text editing facilities within *Imaging* are not really capable of performing large amounts of correcting and layout formatting. It's better to enter your text in a text editor like *WordPad* and then click on the icon to place the pre-typed file directly into your picture.

After clicking on the icon, click on roughly the area you wish to apply the text to and an Open file dialog will open. Choose the text file you wish to use and click **OK**. The text will be placed on the picture in a dotted outline box with nodes at each corner. Click and drag the nodes to size the box and position it by dragging it.

Signature

All great artists sign their work and *Imaging* has a feature which will allow you to sign your work quite easily.

The icon on the extreme right of the lower toolbar is called **Rubber Stamp** and right clicking on it will allow you to choose one of four pre-defined stamps. Choosing **Stamp** and then clicking on the picture will place that stamp on the picture.

Once the stamp has been placed, it can be dragged around to the exact position.

Right clicking on the **Stamp** icon opens a menu, and clicking **Properties** on the menu opens the **Rubber Stamp Properties** dialog which allows you to choose your stamp, edit existing stamps and to create new ones.

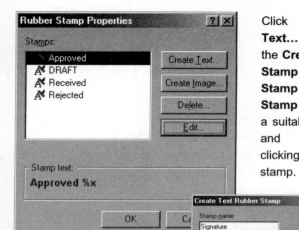

Click on the **Create Text...** button to open the **Create Text Rubber Stamp** dialog. Enter the **Stamp name**, the **Stamp text** and choose a suitable font, font size and colour before clicking **OK** to create the stamp.

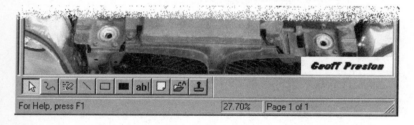

Fame at last. Now it's easy to sign your work: just drag a picture into *Imaging*, select the Signature rubber stamp, stamp it and save it.

A real signature

This signature isn't really a signature, but a name that's been written in a font that looks vaguely reminiscent of handwriting. If you've got a scanner, you can do better.

First, sign your name of a blank piece of paper and scan it at the highest possible resolution. Open it in any of the imaging applications that can crop, and crop the picture, not too tightly, around the signature and save

it as a file called Real Signature, or something similar. Next, open the **Rubber Stamp Properties** dialog and choose **Create Image**. Enter the Stamp name (which must be different from any other stamp name) and then locate the

file of your scanned signature and click on the **OK** box. Now, when you choose your signature as a stamp, you'll get your real signature.

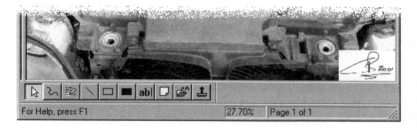

Text effects

Sometimes plain black text is not enough and you start looking for something a little more special. This is fine, but use fancy text with care or it can detract from the picture.

Shadowed text

Creating text with a shadow is a simple way to make it stand out. It can be done in most imaging applications providing the area around the text can be made transparent so that it does not 'overwrite' what's behind. This can be achieved in *Paint*.

Open the picture you wish to label in *Paint*, click the text icon and a window opens in which you select the font characteristics (style, size, etc.).

At the bottom of the left hand tool bar are two icons that determine how additions such as text will be applied. If you want the text to be on a plain background, click the upper icon. If you want the picture to be visible around the text (as in the illustration below), click the lower icon. Move the mouse into the picture, click the left mouse button and type in the text which should be in the colour required for the shadow.

Next, change the colour and select the lower of the two icons on the left of the *Paint* window. This will ensure that when the upper text is placed over the text you have just typed, it will not be obliterated by the background.

When you have entered the text again (this time in a different colour, but with all other settings the same) position it just above and slightly to one side of the first piece of text you entered.

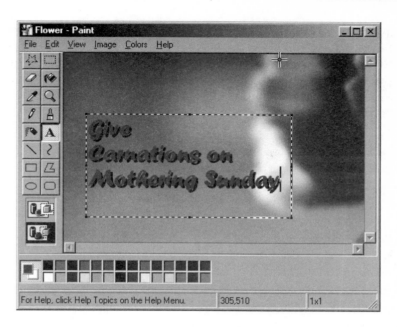

Try to avoid leaving a gap between the nearest text and the shadow text as it can be difficult to read, as is the case here, although it is clearer in colour.

Moulded text

If you've got *PhotoImpact*, you can produce even better text effects.

Click on the text tool on the left hand tool bar and then click the mouse pointer in the picture. A dialog will open into which you can enter a piece of text – a word, phrase, title, etc., and click the **OK** button.

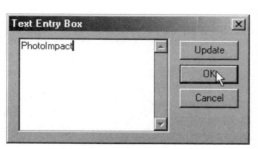

When the text tool is selected, the top toolbar will show several text-related options.

The font name, size and colour are self-explanatory. The style refers to whether the text is in italic, bold or underlined and whether it is to be aligned to the left, right or centre.

Clicking on the arrow on the right opens a menu with 3 entries. For this exercise you should choose Path. The text will appear in outline form and inside a bounding

box. On the bounding are eight nodes, shown here as crosses on the edge on the box. Any or all of the nodes can be dragged in almost any

direction to mould the text into almost any shape. When the text is in the desired shape, click the mouse pointer anywhere away from the text, and it will be drawn in the current foreground colour.

The interesting part about this is that the text is still in text format and still editable. If you click on the text again, the text dialog opens containing the text originally entered. This text can be changed and when the **Update** button is clicked the moulded text will be changed, but the shape of the mould will remain the same.

Coloured and textured text

Sometimes it's preferable to make the text part of the picture rather than a detail that's been added later. *PerfectPhoto* can produce some interesting text effects which, with a little thought, can make some excellent pictures.

The dialog can be found by clicking on **View** on the menubar and choosing **Text...** from the drop down menu. The mouse pointer inherits a new pointer which, when clicked on the picture, opens a dialog.

The dialog allows you to choose the usual features like font, size, style and alignment, but also allows you to choose a different border colour and border thickness.

In addition to having a coloured centre to the font, you can also have a texture. A texture can be any bitmap image supported by *PerfectPhoto*.

From the dialog, choose the texture option and select a suitable file which will become the centre of the text.

Taking this idea a step further, you can choose a transparent centre which enables you to see through the text onto a picture placed behind.

Open the picture you want to use, which will probably need to be much wider than it is high. Use a heavy text and enter it in capitals so that the area that the text covers is as large as possible. Use a medium thickness outline and set the text larger than it needs to be so that you can use a resize tool to make it smaller to fit the picture. (It's better to do it this way round rather than using small text and making it larger.) When you've positioned the text over the picture, choose a medium shade with a 35% transparency and flood fill the area around the text, not forgetting to fill the centres of letters like 'O' and 'D'. This will give a faded effect around the text, but the letters will be in full colour.

Restoring Photos

Cleaning up

Modern cameras make it difficult but not impossible to take a less than perfect picture but occasionally you take a photograph that turns out to have a defect. Scanned images of old pictures can also have photographic flaws caused by either poor equipment or a poor photographer.

Red eye

This used to be a common problem caused by indiscriminate use of flash. The intense flash light bounces off the subject's retina and causes the eyes to glow blood red.

PerfectPhoto includes the facility to correct red eye. Clicking on **View** on the menubar and choosing **Red Eyes...** from the drop down menu opens the dialog.

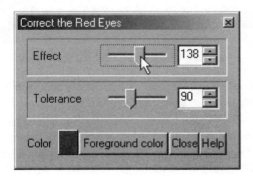

You must choose first choose the correct colour of the eyes. The effect and tolerance can be set between 0 and 255 to determine the range of colours similar to red that will be altered.

Marks

It's amazing how often a carefully composed photograph is spoiled by a blemish that wasn't apparent when the picture was taken. The picture of the car looked fine until viewed on screen when several large pieces of chewing gum appeared on the pavement.

Small marks can like this can be removed in a variety of ways. The smudge tool (see page 91) can work wonders but some applications like *PhotoDeluxe* have a special tool for the purpose.

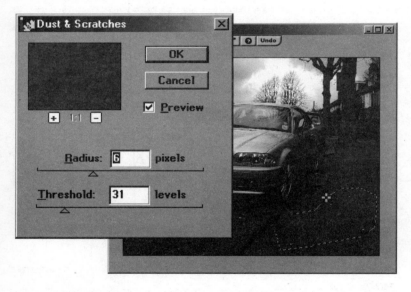

Click on **Effects** on the menubar, go to **Noise** on the drop down menu and choose **Dust and Scratches...** from the sub menu to open the dialog. Mark around the offending blemish (or blemishes if there are several near to each other) and click on **OK** in the dialog. If necessary, the radius of the blemish can be adjusted. The threshold determines how much different the colour of the blemish is from the surrounding area.

Apart from removing chewing gum, this feature works well on old photos that have inherited a lot of scratches and creases.

Morphing

What is Morphing?

The term morphing comes from the word metamorphosis which is the process a caterpillar goes through when it changes to a butterfly. A morphing program is a clever piece of software that changes one picture into another.

There are several morphing applications readily available on the Internet. Visit http://www.zdnet.com/ and enter morphing in the search panel and a list of morphing applications will be displayed. Some of them have to be paid for, but many are free either on a trial basis or permanently.

Morpheus is freeware, which means you can use it free of charge, but you must not use it for any profit making enterprise, nor may you dismantle it and use bits of it in your own software. In fact, you are under exactly the same conditions as with any piece of commercial software.

Getting started

You need to begin with two pictures which should be the same size and similar in composition.

For this morph I've chosen a famous author and his dog.

It would have been better had the backgrounds been similar, but the main features of the two pictures are more alike than you might at first think. Both feature a head, with two eyes, nose and mouth. A pair of pictures, one of which is full face and the other in profile (hence showing only one eye) would not be as easy to work with.

Run *Morpheus* and drag the two pictures into the panels on the left and right of the window. On the right of the *Morpheus* window is a panel into which you must enter the number of frames. This is the total number of frames including the start and end picture. The default number is 3 which means the program will create just 1 frame between the start and end frames.

The way to determine the way a morph creates intermediate frames is much the same for most morphing programs: place nodes on one picture to correspond with nodes on the second picture.

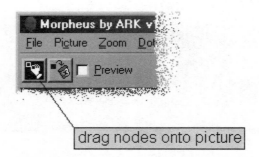

drag nodes onto picture

The nodes are created by clicking the left hand button on the toolbar and dragging into either the start or finish frame. Each time you drag a node into one frame, another corresponding node appears in the other frame. To help you identify which node in one picture belongs to which node in the other picture, they are colour coded.

Begin by placing a node on the tip of the nose, and then aligning the node in the other frame so that too is on the tip of the nose.

Begin by dragging a node onto the nose of the first picture. Then, drag the corresponding node in the other picture to the nose.

It's best to begin with a key feature of the subject. In the case of morphs involving people, I always find it's best to place the first node on the end of the nose, then do the corners of the eyes, then the corners of the mouth and gradually build up the number of nodes in the picture. The more nodes you use, the better the morph will be.

You can view intermediate frames as you go to check how well it's working.

Who said a dog owner looks like his dog? These ten frames are the result of the morph outlined in the preceding pages. More nodes and more frames would have resulted in a smoother morph, but there is a price: the size of the file increases dramatically. Larger pictures could also have led to a better output.

Most morphing programs allow you to output either a movie or a series of still pictures. Morpheus is typical in that it will output either a series of bitmap pictures with filename *filename*001, *filename*002, etc., and AVI movie files.

AVI is the standard format for moving images in Windows and these files can be played in a variety of applications, including Windows Media Player which is supplied with Microsoft Windows.

The filmstrip was created by drawing a black square and adding some white rectangles to represent the holes which the projector drive sprockets engage on. A hole was cut out of the rectangle and the morphed pictures were then placed behind.

If you want to see what your son or daughter will look like when they're older, try morphing a picture of yourself with one of your child.

Galleries & Albums

Catalogue and display

Many imaging applications have their own gallery to store and display
pictures or clips. These are often a more convenient way of keeping
track of your work than trying to wade through the folders in My
Pictures.

When a picture is saved from *PhotoDeluxe* and the Save dialog is
displayed, you'll notice that at the bottom is an additional section entitled
Add to Gallery.

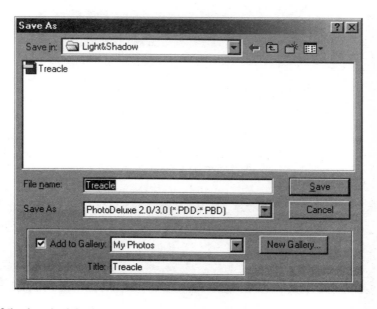

If the box is ticked, then information about the file (not the file itself, just
the information about its whereabouts) will be saved in the Gallery. It will

be saved with the same name as the filename (although it can be changed) and will be added to the designated gallery.

You can have as many galleries in the Gallery as you wish and new galleries can be added at anytime by clicking the **New Gallery...** button and entering the name for the new gallery in the box.

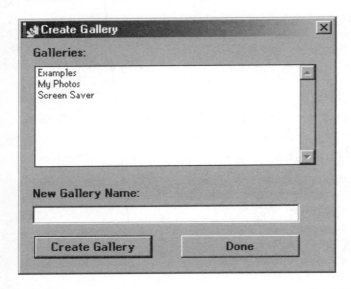

To call up the Gallery, click on **File** on the menubar, go to **My Photos** on the drop down menu and choose **Show My Photos** on the sub menu.

You can only display compatible files in *EasyPhoto*, ie pictures that can be read by *PhotoDeluxe*.

Double clicking one of the pictures will open it in *PhotoDeluxe* provided the file hasn't been moved to another location or renamed. The important point to remember about *My Photos* is that it doesn't save pictures. It merely stores information about their location. The gallery file that is created is therefore very small.

When the application is first installed it comes with three galleries: **Examples**, **My Photos** and **Screen Saver**. File information saved in the latter can be used as a system screen saver. This is explained later in the chapter.

The application used by *PhotoDeluxe* to create the Galleries is *EasyPhoto* and this application can be accessed without going into *PhotoDeluxe*. When *PhotoDeluxe* was installed a shortcut was added to the Start Menu. Alongside that shortcut should be another shortcut to *EasyPhoto*.

When *EasyPhoto* is started from the Start Menu shortcut, all galleries are displayed vertically. File information about individual photos can be copied between the galleries and information about the files edited.

EasyPhoto has yet another trick: a full screen slide show where the pictures in a particular gallery are displayed one after the other. To start the slide show, click

on **File** on the menubar and choose **Display Gallery as Slide Show** from the drop down menu.

PerfectPhoto also has an album which can be accessed by clicking on the button in the top right hand corner of the *PerfectPhoto* window. The same button appears in the Album and the Gallery enabling you to quickly switch between them.

Pictures can be dragged into the Album but as with *EasyPhoto*, it's only the information about the picture that is saved and not the picture itself.

You can create as many albums as you wish and they can be easily selected by clicking on the Open button on the button bar at the top of the screen.

Double clicking on a thumbnail opens it in the *PerfectPhoto* image editor.

Screen saver

Some applications can add images to a screen saver. The idea behind a screen saver is that if the computer is not being used for several hours, having the same picture on the screen can damage it. A screen saver is a way of preventing damage by displaying a constantly changing image.

The screen savers generated by photo editing applications take the form of a slide show with a selection of pictures displayed for a few seconds before changing to a new picture.

PhotoDeluxe can create a screen saver. Click on **File** on the menubar, go to **Export** on the drop down menu and choose **Screen Saver...** from the sub menu. This will store the file information in a special folder within *EasyPhoto* called Screen Saver.

You can get exactly the same result when you save a picture from *PhotoDeluxe* by choosing the Screen Saver gallery from the Save dialog.

The first time you create a screen saver using this method, the software should automatically configure your computer so that the screen save is active. If it doesn't, or you want to adjust any of the settings, open the **Window Display Properties** dialog. This can be found by clicking the **Start** button at the bottom left of the computer screen which opens the **Start Menu**, going to **Settings** and choosing **Control Panel** from the sub menu. When the Control Panel opens, double click **Display** which opens the **Display Properties** dialog and click the **Screen Saver** tab at the top of the dialog.

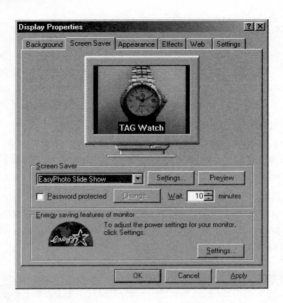

Choose **EasyPhoto Slide Show** from the list of screen savers which can be found by clicking the downward pointing arrow in the Screen Saver panel. Clicking on the **Settings** button opens a further dialog which allows you to choose whether to display the captions with the pictures or not.

This is an excellent way to display your pictures, but you can view even more of them if you put several together in one file. Create a blank document, place four pictures into it, scale them down so that they all fit into the document and save it.

Projects

Things to do

The obvious thing to do with photographs is to print them out on paper and frame them or mount them in an album like conventional photographs. But there are alternatives.

Calendar

Many people give a calendar to friends as a gift at the end of the year. If you want to give a really special calendar, make it yourself and include some of your photos on it.

PerfectPhoto and *PhotoDeluxe* both feature a calendar creation option where you can include some of your own pictures to decorate it.

The *PhotoDeluxe* version is accessed by clicking on **Cards & More** on the menubar and choosing **Calendars**.

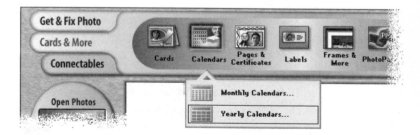

This application offers either monthly calendars or a yearly calendar, and these are selected from the drop down menu. From there on, it's simply a case of making a choice from each of the numbered steps. You can choose the style and then make adjustments to it, choose any additional decoration and then add your own picture.

All of the elements of the calendar pages are stored on separate layers so it's easy to move bits around to get it exactly right. Creating a calendar in *PhotoDeluxe* creates a new document which can be saved and then loaded and printed at a later date.

PerfectPhoto also creates a new document when you create a calendar. The calendar option can be found by clicking on **Image** on the menubar and choosing **Calendar** from the drop down menu.

This version of a calendar creator doesn't include lots of fancy cartoon graphics like *PhotoDeluxe*, but it does give you a degree of control over the fonts used for the various textual elements of the calendar. These include the choice of font colours, the option of an outline for the month and year, Sundays printed in a different colour, holidays printed in another different colour and text to describe holiday dates.

Of course you can also import your own picture and adjust its size and position.

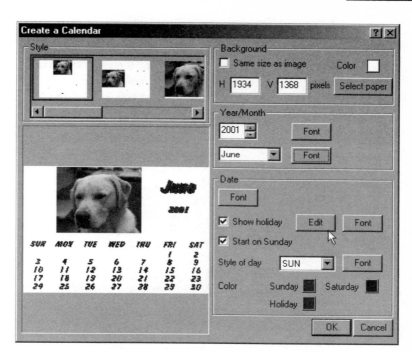

Each of the styles chosen from the top left section of the dialog can be adjusted by hand, but if you are going to make a set of one-page calendars ensure there is a degree of uniformity between them.

Purpose built

The calendar creation options in *PhotoDeluxe* and *PerfectPhoto* are rather like extensions to the application whose main job is editing digital images. But there are purpose built calendar creation applications available, some of which are very cheap.

Greenstreet's *CalendarMaker2* is one such program that is designed to create calendars and nothing else. Just about everything that you would want to do to create a calendar is possible, including creating a desktop diary.

When the program starts you are presented with a window which steers you through the process. In the first screen you simply choose the year. Click the arrow at the bottom right to move onto the next screen which asks for the type of diary or calendar: monthly, annual or quarterly. You can also choose the style from the standard designs supplied and whether you want weeks to begin on a Sunday or Monday, or any other day.

The next screen gives you the chance to enter any additional data like your name or business name, and the period you want the calendar for.

The next screen is where you can insert a picture. *CalendarMaker2* is supplied with a huge library of images, but most people will want to import their own. Choosing the **Import** button (fourth icon from left) opens the familiar **Open file** dialog from where you choose a file to insert in your calendar. If your calendar has more than one page you can choose a different picture for each page, and if two pictures are required on a page, they can different..

Once the Calendar has been created, there's not a great deal that can be done with it unless you have Greenstreet's *Publisher4* which allows you to resize the images and change the font style, size and colour.

A great way to use pictures is to create your own calendars. Grandparents would love to have a calendar like this featuring their grandchildren.

This is a an excellent project for children to undertake as it need not take a long time to create, and the results are always very professional looking.

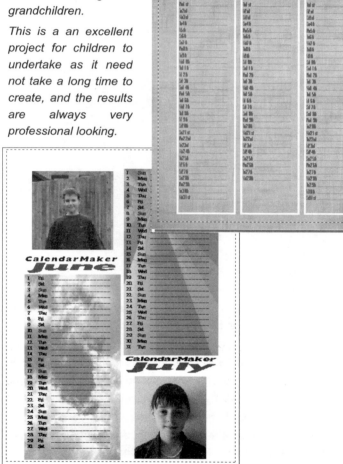

Cross stitch

Counted cross stitch is a type of embroidery which sadly is not as popular as it once was. If you have a really special picture, you can turn it into a cross stitch pattern and stitch it.

There are several programs that will convert pictures into cross-stitch patterns, but few are as easy to use *as Jane Greenoff''s Cross Stitch Creator* by Focus Multimedia which costs less than £10. (Full details about where to buy this application can be found in Appendix 3 on page 287.)

If you've never tried counted cross stitch before, you should not be too ambitious for your first attempt so begin by choosing a simple picture which should also be quite small.

Crop it as tightly as possible and if the picture has a busy background, it might be worth using a selection tool to remove it so you are just left with the main subject. (The section on selecting on page 131 and cropping on page 145 explain these processes fully.)

When you've got your picture ready, run the cross stitch application, click on **File** on the menubar and choose **Import** from the drop down menu.

You'll be asked to locate the file you wish to use and this process is fully explained in the section on loading and saving on page 25.

The Import Wizard dialog then opens the picture and, based on its current size, will calculate how many stitches will be required horizontally and vertically. You may change these figures but note that changing one of the values will automatically change the other by the same proportion in order to keep the aspect ratio the same. (See the Glossary on page 277 for a description of the aspect ratio.)

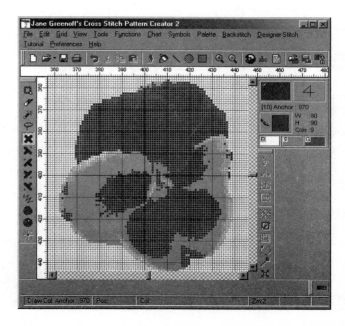

Remember, the total number of stitches required for the pattern are the two numbers multiplied together (assuming there are no blank spaces and that there is a stitch in every row of every column).

Click **Next** and choose the number of colours you wish to use in the pattern. You'll need to refer to the original for this, but 10 is a reasonable figure to begin with.

Click **Next** and choose which brand and type of thread you wish to use. There are lots of choices, depending on what you want to make. It could be something the size of a postcard or a floor rug!

Finally the picture is imported and converted into a pattern.

You may find you need to do a little tidying up. The pansy produced the pattern (shown on the previous page) using 10 colours, but one of the colours was used for just 1 stitch. Needless to say, that colour was replaced with one of the other nine.

This pattern requires 80 x 90 stitches, which is a total of 720 stitches, however the area immediately surrounding the flower is blank and so it's more like 550 stitches.

When you're a little more experienced with this type of needlework you might try something a little larger, but be aware of what you're taking on. An unedited 800 x 640 pixel picture produces a cross stitch pattern of over half a million stitches. Using 18 gauge fabric (18 stitches to the inch) will produce a finished work of almost 4ft x 3ft. If you could do 4 stitches per minute it would take over 1700 hours. Quite a project, but what a beautiful piece of work you'll have at the end.

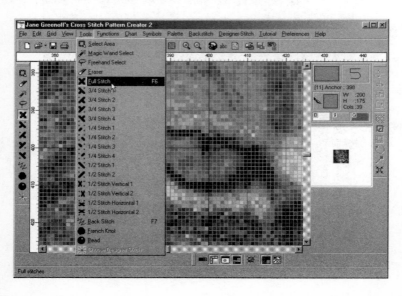

The pattern of Emma the cat was generated from a photograph 800 x 640, but when the number of vertical and horizontal stitches were calculated, the numbers were more than halved giving a final pattern size of 300 x 240 making 72,000 stitches: a much more manageable project. The colours were restricted to 50.

Once the pattern has been generated you can, if you wish, enter the types of stitch.

The final pattern should be printed in colour and will usually fill several sheets. If you haven't got a colour printer the colours can be converted to symbols and a key generated.

Greetings cards

Like calendars, software for printing greetings cards is quite common. Also like calendars, receiving a personalised card which has been carefully designed is greatly appreciated. More so than buying an 'off-the-shelf' card at an inflated price.

Print&Go by Image-Pro is a simple yet effective program which will enable you to easily design and print lovely cards for any occasion on special pre-folded card.

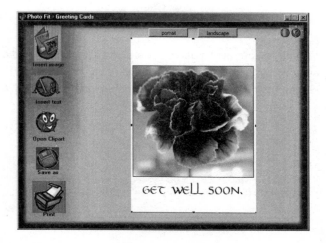

Like the other software featured in this book, it's cheap. When *Print&Go* is run, a window opens with five icons down the left side. Clicking each in turn from the top to the bottom takes you through the processes needed to create your card: Import a picture, Add some text, Add some clipart (optional), Save and Print.

There isn't much scope to alter the card once you've incorporated the elements, although you can change the font and font size. If you want more control, *PhotoDeluxe* has a card creation feature which is accessed via the toolbar at the top. Choose **Cards & More** and then whichever type of card you wish to create from the drop down menu.

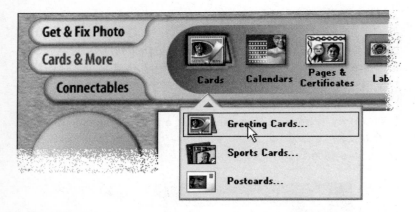

You first must decide which pattern of card you want to use, and this will be determined by the card you intend printing on. You have a choice of four patterns, some of which can be printed onto paper as thin as $140g/m^2$.

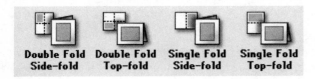

Next you are asked to choose the design of card; most of which have one or more ready made spaces to include your own photos.

It is at this stage you can, if you wish, add your own photographs. Most designs require a picture for the front and one or two for the inside. Any text that is provided on the card template can also be altered at this stage.

When you've added all the components to the card template, you'll almost certainly need to make some fine adjustments to it. All the elements of the card will have been placed on separate layers (see the section on layers on page 177) making it easy to adjust. In particular, the photos may need to be scaled, or as in the case in the example below, altered so they can fit into a pre-defined, but irregular space.

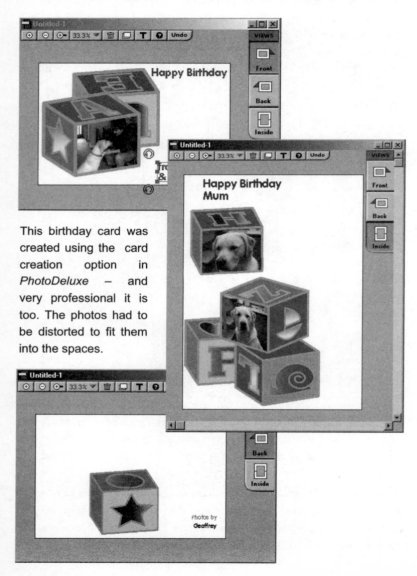

This birthday card was created using the card creation option in *PhotoDeluxe* – and very professional it is too. The photos had to be distorted to fit them into the spaces.

What else?

If you use a digital camera you have the potential to generate an enormous number of pictures. Even if you discard 75% of them, you'll still have a lot of pictures left. Printing them and putting them into an album or framing them is an obvious way to use your pictures but you could create a library to view on your computer. With a little imagination you can do a lot more with them.

You can have a great deal of fun playing around with them, incorporating bits from one picture into another, or you can display your pictures in unusual ways.

Apart from the calendar, cross stitch pattern and greetings cards described in this section, there's also the T Shirt design which is outlined on page 219 and the origami boxes on page 152.

These are just half-a-dozen ideas which should get you started. At this stage you're merely limited by your own imagination.

Appendix 1

Glossary of Terms

Anti-Aliasing. A means of fogging the edges of a curved line to try to fool the eye into thinking it's smoother than it actually is. Pixels in varying shades are applied to the edge of curved and diagonal lines to improve their on-screen appearance.

Aspect Ratio. The ratio of height to width. It is important to maintain the aspect ratio of a picture if you wish to keep pictures in proportion.

Attributes. The properties of (usually) an image. The information will include size, resolution, depth of colour, etc.

Backup. A copy of a file which is saved for security purposes – if something happens to the file you're working on, you can use the backup so you don't lose your work.

Bit Mapped. A bit mapped image is one where each of the pixels is given a colour.

BMP. Bit mapped file - the standard file format for Windows. Many applications can load a BMP image, but *Paint*, which is supplied with Windows, is the default program for this filetype.

bpp. Bits per pixel. The amount of information about each pixel in an image. 1 bit per pixel means that each pixel may be either black or white. With 2 bpp, each pixel can be any one of 4 colours. 4bpp = 16 colours.

Clipboard. A section of computer memory that can temporarily hold a document or part of a document.

Compression. Compressing a file reduces the amount of memory it consumes. Some file formats have compression built in. Others can be compressed by varying amounts during saving but the trade-off is size against quality.

Copy. Make a duplicate file or part of a file and store it in the clipboard. Most programs allow the shortcut *CTRL C* to copy the currently selected section of text or graphic (or the whole text or graphic if no selection has been made).

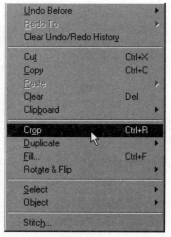

Crop. Remove the unwanted edges of a photograph so that the main subject remains. The resulting cropped picture will usually still be rectangular (or square) and will be smaller. As a result, it will also occupy less memory.

Cut. Exactly the same as *Copy*, except the original is removed. Most programs allow *CTRL X* as a shortcut.

CMYK. A method of describing colours which is preferred by printers. Each colour is described in terms of Cyan, Magenta, Yellow and Black.

Dialog. A pop-up panel containing information but also having input panels for the user to enter values.

Drag and Drop. A means of opening a file into an application by dragging it from a filer window and into a program window.

Drop down menu. Clicking a name on the menubar will open a menu containing items relating to the name. Eg, click *File* and a menu will open containing entries like *Load, Save, Save as,* etc.

Filename. The name given to a file when saving. Any combination of letters or numbers may be used up to a total of 255 characters. Some symbols such as ?/~. may not be used. It makes sense to use a name that has some meaning to the picture. eg *Children at Brighton July 1999* has some meaning whereas *10045a* could be anything.

Filesize. The amount of space a document occupies on the backing storage (hard disc, floppy disc) or in the internal memory.

Filetype. The format the file is held in. For graphics, there are dozens of different formats, but JPEG, BMP and TIFF are the most widely used.

Filer window. A window which provides a view of folders and files on a storage medium like a hard disc or floppy disc.

GIF. Graphics Interchange Format. A bit-mapped file type which is a particularly popular format for web images.

High colour. The attributes for each pixel are described in 16 bits or 2 bytes (each bit being a binary digit capable of being set to 1 or 0). There are 65,536 combinations of 16 bits which relate to 65,536 different colours.

Icon. A small graphic which has a meaning or represents something. In the case of files or documents, a file icon represents a filetype. Double clicking on the icon in a filer window will open the application that is associated with that filetype. eg Double clicking on a Word document will start Word and open the document into it ready for editing or printing.

JPEG. Joint Photographic Experts Group. The preferred file format for true colour photographs.

Landscape. A picture or paper having the longest side horizontally. See *Orientation*.

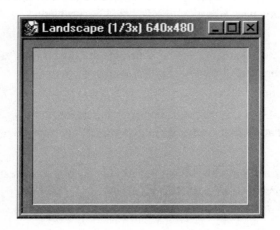

Layers. Placing various elements of a picture on different levels. This process enables various elements to be moved in front of, or behind other objects.

Marquee. A selected part of an image surrounded by a dashed line.

Mask. A feature used in some photo editing applications which allows you to work on one area whilst protecting another area close to the area being edited.

Menubar. The row of labels across the top of a window. Clicking on one opens a menu.

Multi-tasking. The ability of an application to handle more than one document simultaneously.

Object. A selected area of a picture which can be moved and edited quite separately from the rest of the picture.

Orientation. The way the paper is oriented (positioned). Landscape has the longest size horizontal, whilst portrait has the longest side vertical.

Paste. Transfers the current contents of the clipboard into the currently active document. Most programs allow *CTRL V* as a shortcut.

Pixel. A picture element: the smallest point on a screen that can be assigned a colour.

Pixelation. When a bit-mapped image is enlarged, the pixels are represented by larger squares. In this form, curves and diagonal lines no longer look smooth, but become very jagged, or pixelated.

Portrait. A picture or paper having the longest side vertically. See *Orientation*.

ppi. The resolution of a picture described in pixels per inch.

Properties. Clicking the right hand mouse button over a file icon in a filer window opens a menu. Selecting *Properties* opens an information window showing the filetype, size, when last accessed, when modified, etc.

Resolution. The number of pixels displayed in a given linear distance. The higher the number, the smaller the physical dimensions of the picture.

RGB. A common method of describing colours is by the amount of Red, Green and Blue they contain.

Selection. Marking or selecting a piece of text or an area of graphics so that it can be worked on separately or pasted into another program.

TIFF. Tagged Image File Format. A graphics format popular with the print industry.

Transparent background. A background that is not white but can be seen through revealing what, if anything, is behind.

True colour. The attributes for each pixel are described in 24 bits or 3 bytes (each bit being a binary digit capable of being set to 1 or 0). There are 16,777,216 combinations of 24 bits which relates to 16,777,216 different colours.

Undo. Refers to the last action carried out on a file. Applications usually have this on the *Edit* menu, but in most cases, *CTRL Z* will undo the last action and put the file back to the state it was in before the last action was performed on it. *SHIFT CTRL Z* will often undo the last undo, whilst further undo commands will undo previous editing.

Vector Graphics. A computer generated drawing which is stored as a collection of formulae, rather than simply rows of coloured pixels. The advantage of vector graphics is that drawings can be resized without any loss of quality, unlike bit-mapped graphics which suffer from loss of quality when scaled up or down.

WinZip. An application to compress files. Bit-mapped pictures compress particularly well, usually resulting in a file occupying less than half the uncompressed size on disc. If you intend sending pictures via email, compressing them makes the mailing much smaller and hence much faster. WinZip can be downloaded from http://www.winzip.com/

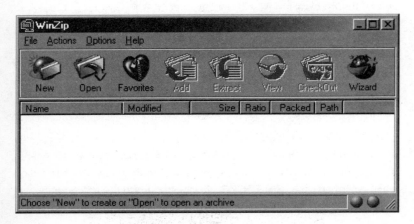

Appendix 2

Comparative sizes

How big?

- A sheet of A4 paper is 21.0cms x 29.7cms or in inches, about 8¼" x 11¾".

- At 72dpi that's 595 pixels x 842 pixels.

- If the resolution is increased to 144dpi the paper size becomes 10.5cms x 14.85cms.

- In 24 bit colour, it will occupy 1,468Kbytes in memory, but if you save it as a BMP file, it won't fit on a standard 3½" High-Density floppy disc.

- If it was saved in JPEG format with moderate compression it would occupy less than 8½ Kbytes. Even with no compression it would only occupy 16Kbytes.

- A 256-colour BMP file would occupy 491Kbytes on disc.

- Uncompressed, this 1768 x 1312 JPEG file…

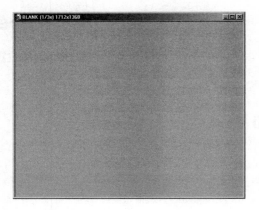

BLANK (1/3x) 1712x1368

... occupies the same disc space as this one which is exactly the same size and resolution, and set for the same colour depth.

- An image occupies the same memory regardless of its orientation.

- Reducing the physical dimensions of a picture by 50% reduces the amount of memory it occupies to ¼ of its original size.

- Scaling a picture so that it appears larger or smaller on the screen does not affect the amount of disc space it occupies.

- Files which contain additional information like layers, require much more memory as they contain information about areas that may be hidden.

Appendix 3

Useful Addresses

Featured Programs

This book focuses on five programs which were supplied free of charge with either hardware or software products. More information about the five programs, including details of how to buy the full versions are available from the companies' websites.

PhotoDeluxe by **Adobe**

Web: http://www.adobe.com/

PhotoHouse by **Corel**

Web: http://www.corel.com/

PerfectPhoto by **IBM**

Web: http://www.ibm.com/

PhotoEditor by **Microsoft**

Web: http://www.microsoft.com/

PhotoImpact by **ULead**

Web: http://www.ulead.com/

Other Software

Apart from the five key programs, other software is mentioned which is either supplied free with other hardware or software products, or for which there is a small charge. In most cases, the chargeable software featured in this book costs less than £15.

Imaging by **Kodak**

Web: http://www.kodak.com/

Jane Greenoff's Cross Stitch Pattern Creator 2 by **Focus**

Focus Multimedia Ltd
The Studios
Lea Hall Enterprise Park
Armitage Road
Rugeley
Staffordshire WS15 1LH

Phone: 01889 570156
Fax: 01889 583571
Web: http://www.focusmm.co.uk/

Morpheus by ARK

Download from…

Email: rubleyr@river.it.gvsu.edu

PhotoFX, PhotoFX2 and **CalendarCreator2** by **Greenstreet**

Greenstreet software
PO Box 62
St Ives
Cambridgeshire PE27 4RY

Phone: 01480 496789
Fax: 01480 496189
Web: http://www.gstsoft.com/

PhotoShop by **Adobe**

Web: http://www.adobe.com/

Printer Supplies

Printer papers and card specially for colour inkjet printers are available from the following retailers...

Epson

Web: http://www/epson.com/

Hewlett Packard

Web: http://www.hp.com/

ImagePro

Phone: 0845 603 0016
Fax: 0845 603 0017
Web: http://www.inkjetsupplies.com/
Email: imagepro@inkjetsupplies.com

Ryman

Web: http://www.ryman.co.uk/

Vista Papers

Freepost (LE6296)
Hinckley LE10 0BR

Phone: 0800 616244
Fax: 0800 716563
Web: http://www.vistapapers.co.uk/
Email: sales@vistapapers.co.uk

Remote Storage

Some websites offer free picture storage.

Internet Cameras Direct

Web: http://www.internetcamerasdirect.co.uk/

Hardware

In addition to the standard computer kit (keyboard, monitor, printer, mouse, etc.), a couple of useful additions are included in the book.

Aisin POEM Embroidery Machine

Techsoft UK Ltd
The Grange
Eryrys
Mold
Denbighshire CH7 4DB

Phone: 01824 780318
Fax: 01824 780564
Web: http://www.techsoftuk.co.uk/
Email: email@techsoftuk.co.uk

Jessops

Web: http://www.jessops.co.uk/

Wacom Graphics Tablet

Web: http://www.wacom.com/

Website

Many of the pictures contained in this book really need to be seen in colour to fully appreciate them.

To enable you to see them in colour, I have placed many of them on my website...

www.word4word.uk.com/imaging.html

or go to...

www.word4word.uk.com/

and click on the *Easy PC Digital Imaging* book cover.

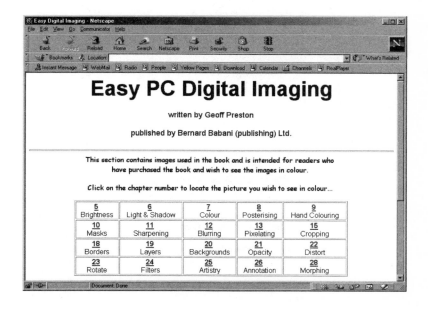

Website

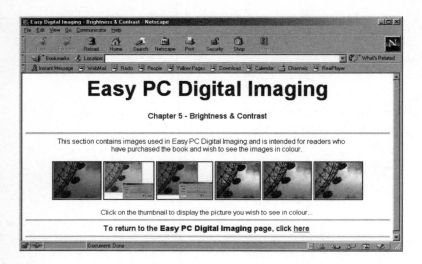

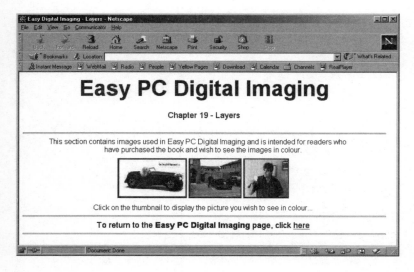

The author is fully responsible for maintaining the Word4Word website. The publishers of this book accept no responsibility for the quality of the images provided, or in respect of any damage or injury that might be suffered or caused by their use. The publishers do not guarantee in any way, the continued accessibility of this site.

Main Index

Featured Software Index